Internet Popular Culture and (Everyday) Politics

This edited collection considers how scholars conduct research on (everyday) politics in Southeast Asia via networks of internet popular culture. This includes artefacts, networks, groups, and cultures that are specific to Southeast Asian online practices, and that seek to represent, advocate for, provoke, or question how citizens "do" politics online.

In the Southeast Asia region in particular, these behind-the-scenes minutiae of everyday decisions are all the more under-valued when researchers have been taught, conditioned, or cautioned to tiptoe around taboo or political topics implicitly policed by states and governments. The combination of media regimes with limited press freedoms, the employment of sedition acts against citizens, and the need to be strategic to secure state and industry funding for research have pressured or motivated scholars to strategically obscure certain research anecdotes in favour of a smoother publishing journey and/or posterity. As such, this collection serves as a sounding board and collection of reflections on what it really looks like to conduct research on everyday politics online in the Southeast Asian region, while navigating innovative media methods, negotiating interdisciplinary gatekeeping, demands of publishing in tiered journals, and the tensions around legitimising one's methodological choices. This collection features four accounts of scholars contemplating the methodological and ethical conundrums when conducting research on Southeast Asian internet popular culture and everyday politics.

This book will be useful for the readers in the disciplines of anthropology, Asian studies, communications, cultural studies, media studies, and science and technology studies.

Crystal Abidin (PhD) is Professor of Internet Studies at Curtin University. She is Director of the Influencer Ethnography Research Lab and Founder of the TikTok Cultures Research Network. Crystal is a digital anthropologist focusing on social media pop cultures especially in the Asia Pacific region. Reach her at wishcrys. com.

Natalie Pang (PhD) is Head and Associate Professor in the Department of Communications and New Media, National University of Singapore. Her research lies at the intersection of technology and society, and her research projects are organised under the themes of digital citizenship, inclusion and well-being.

Internet Popular Culture and (Everyday) Politics

Methodological & Ethical Critiques
from Southeast Asia

**Edited by Crystal Abidin
and Natalie Pang**

Routledge
Taylor & Francis Group
LONDON AND NEW YORK

First published 2026
by Routledge
4 Park Square, Milton Park, Abingdon, Oxon OX14 4RN

and by Routledge
605 Third Avenue, New York, NY 10158

Routledge is an imprint of the Taylor & Francis Group, an informa business

British Library Cataloguing-in-Publication Data
A catalogue record for this book is available from the British Library

ISBN: 978-1-041-02465-1 (hbk)
ISBN: 978-1-041-02467-5 (pbk)
ISBN: 978-1-003-61936-9 (ebk)

DOI: 10.4324/9781003619369

Typeset in Times New Roman
by KnowledgeWorks Global Ltd.

Crystal: To Uncle Murad, for role-modelling a
melting pot of cultures.

Natalie: To Mum, who seeded all my curiosity about
identities and Southeast Asia.

Contents

Figures and Tables

Figures

Table

About the Editors

Crystal Abidin (PhD) is Professor of Internet Studies at Curtin University. She is Director of the Influencer Ethnography Research Lab and Founder of the TikTok Cultures Research Network. Crystal is a digital anthropologist focusing on social media pop cultures especially in the Asia Pacific region. Reach her at wishcrys.com.

Natalie Pang (PhD) is Head and Associate Professor in the Department of Communications and New Media, National University of Singapore. Her research lies at the intersection of technology and society, and her research projects are organised under the themes of digital citizenship, inclusion and well-being.

Contributors

Samuel I. Cabbuag is a PhD Candidate in the Department of Sociology at Hong Kong Baptist University and an Assistant Professor in the Department of Sociology at the University of the Philippines Diliman. His research focuses on Southeast Asian digital cultures. Reach him at sicabbuag@up.edu.ph.

Fajar Junaedi is an Associate Professor and Researcher in the Communication Department, Universitas Muhammadiyah Yogyakarta, Indonesia. He has been researching football fans in Indonesia, particularly in relation to communication studies for more than 15 years. He has written several books and articles about football fans in Indonesia.

Pauline Pooi Yin Leong (PhD, Monash University) heads the School of Communication and Media Studies at Sunway University, Malaysia. Her research interests are digital media and politics, and media literacy. She is the author of *Malaysian Politics in the New Media Age: Implications on the Political Communication Process*.

Jonathan Corpus Ong (PhD, Cambridge University) is Professor of Global Digital Media at the University of Massachusetts in Amherst, USA. He is the Founding Director of the Global Technology for Social Justice Lab (www.glotechlab.net), which supports engaged research and tech justice advocacy for the Global South.

Muria Endah Sokowati is an Associate Professor of the Magister Program of Media and Communication, Universitas Muhammadiyah Yogyakarta, Indonesia. She is an expert in Media studies with research interests in popular cultures, digital cultures, gender and sexuality, youth culture, and critical theories. She has published books and journal articles on media issues.

Acknowledgements

The editorship towards this book was supported by a Facebook Integrity Foundational Research Award for the project "Decoding the Weaponizing of Pop Culture on WhatsApp in Singapore and Malaysia." The funding of open access of the book was supported by the National University of Singapore, Faculty of Arts and Social Sciences.

Introduction

A Look at Internet Popular Culture and (Everyday) Politics in Southeast Asia

Crystal Abidin and Natalie Pang

Methodological and Ethical Critiques from Southeast Asia

In this collection, we invited scholars to reflect on the methodological and ethical processes and critiques of conducting research on internet popular culture and (everyday) politics in Southeast Asian nations, paying special attention to a decolonising perspective (Duara, 2004). The contributions explored angles including: How theoretical concepts and research practice mutually and reflexively inform each other; the interpretive flexibility and ethical choices that surround the application and usage of information and communication technologies (ICTs) and digital networks to pursue research; and how the hyphen in "socio-technical" manifests in their own work. This refers to research that moves away from technological deterministic assumptions and conclusions but is also careful not to substitute "one form of determinism (technical) with another (social)" (Williams and Edge, 1996). For instance, getting interviewees to share their encounters and reflections on laws on fake news in various societies requires the deployment of different strategies.

In our approach, we prompted contributors to consider the following provocations: What does it really look like to research (everyday) politics online in your country as a fieldsite? How does this matter when navigating topics that are implicitly policed by states and governments (Lyons and Gomez, 2005)? What strategies are required amidst limited press freedoms (Gunaratne, 1999)? How are researchers concerned when states use sedition acts against citizens (International Commission of Jurists, 2014)? How is internet popular culture invoked in these situations? As scholars from and/ or of these Southeast Asian nations, under what socio-cultural, political, and ethical regimes do you have to operate to do your research? Considering the dilemmas of delicate socio-political terrain, what interesting findings emerged from your data that will likely be difficult to publish about? And finally, what does ethical research look like in your fieldsite? Contributor responses are surmised in the section below.

DOI: 10.4324/9781003619369-1

This Collection

This collection features four methodological accounts of scholars contemplating the methodological and ethical conundrums when conducting research on Southeast Asian internet popular culture and everyday politics. Spanning the disciplines of anthropology, Asian studies, communications, cultural studies, media studies, and science and technology studies, the book presents brief summaries of the larger project; functioning as primers to the platformed, cultural, and socio-political context of the study; points to some of the tensions and roadblocks faced by the scholars; and offers strategies, workarounds, and reflections on research practices.

We begin with a chapter on Malaysia by Pauline Pooi Yin Leong, titled "Exploring Methodological Issues in Studying Contentious Communication on Malaysian Social Media." In two projects on contentious communication via the use of political satire, trolling, and hate speech among Malaysian citizens as played out on YouTube and the news portal *Malaysiakini*, Leong highlights the importance of curating an equipped research team. The cultural context of Malaysia presents a culturally, linguistically, and religious diverse field, and socio-political context includes legal stipulations that limit free speech or regulate what is accepted speech. As such, to avoid logistical constraints in data collection, the chapter offers that an effective research team should comprise insiders and outsiders to the subject matter, with a range of cultural and language competencies, as the "identity and contextual positionality" of the team shapes data collection and analytical decisions.

Much has been written about the researcher's gaze since Foucault first conceptualised the notion through his writings about the panopticon, a circular prison where the guards who are located in its centre had constant surveillance of the inmates (Foucault, 1975, 1980). The gaze involves "the making visible of a person or population" (Fox, 1993, p. 24), and in doing so, researchers develop proficiency but also control over the narratives associated with the person or population they are observing. In Indonesia, Muria Endah Sokowati and Fajar Junaedi turn their gaze on one particular underground music community, the *Lamidet* Society, offering insights on how this hidden population utilizes various digital platforms to advocate for the marginalized urban poor through music. The authors explain how social media platforms have become grounds for displaying resistance against a historical backdrop of political dictatorship, a legacy of active political participation by underground musicians and fans, and escalating tensions with the authorities. In doing so, the authors demonstrate how the researcher's gaze is located within its historical and social context, but at the same time, socially constructed.

In the next stage of research management, the chapter on the Philippines underscores the importance of making strategic and ethical decisions when selecting research questions. "Pseudonymous Influencers and Horny 'Alts' in the Philippines: Media Manipulation Be Media Manipulation Beyond 'Fake

News'" by Jonathan Corpus Ong and Samuel Cabbuag, focuses on social media conversations and disinformation narratives during the 2019 Philippines elections, especially as they unfolded on news pages, Instagram, and Twitter. The authors outline the evolving cultural context of the country, including the rapidly expanding ecology of "pseudonymous influencers," such as parody accounts, meme pages, romantic love quote accounts, and horny queer "alt" accounts. It is against these developments that the socio-political context becomes nuanced, as competitive disinformation economies emerge where for-hire influencers can be deployed to peddle political messaging. As such, the study demonstrates some methodological tensions, including the limitations of deploying the frame of "disinformation" to study pseudonymous influencers because fact-checking efforts are limited. The chapter offers that while platform content moderations are slow to understand emerging "cultural nuances of local humor or niche subcultures," research can focus on mapping these newly erupting typologies in the ecology, which can then be translated into pragmatic suggestions to patch regulatory loopholes.

Finally, we turn to Singapore where authors Crystal Abidin and Natalie Pang outline the team's selection of their analytical approach, in their multi-sited study of citizens and diaspora/migrants in WhatsApp family chatgroups against the backdrop of pandemic misinformation. Titled "Studying Private Messaging Groups: Misinformation in WhatsApp Family Groupchats, and Research Regimes in Singapore(ans)," the authors outline the cultural context where family and health advocacy groups are fast proliferating on WhatsApp specifically to negotiate and disseminate family values, and where WhatsApp use is also becoming prominent among the elderly Boomers as a "first stop" for information dissemination from the government. In the socio-political context where society is highly shaped by technological innovations and developments, WhatsApp has become normatively used for "networks of care." However, the authors struggled with data solicitation as participants appeared to have internalized values and norms propagated by the state, and reportage in personal interviews was often shrouded in "'textbook' answers" as permissible speak. In response, the study deployed the scroll back method (Robards and Lincoln, 2017) as a way to "'safely' challenge and question the participant's recall, truth-making, and sense-making." In the analysis, the chapter reiterates the need to frame such studies to be ethnographic by design, by focusing on "voices and perspectives from the 'margins'" through purposive sampling, and being attentive to "'decoding' doublespeak and code switching" in the analysis of interview transcripts.

Acknowledgements

The production of this collection was supported by a 2019 Facebook Integrity Foundational Research Award for a project titled "Decoding the Weaponizing of Pop Culture on WhatsApp in Singapore and Malaysia." The funding of open access costs of the book was supported by the National University of Singapore, Faculty of Arts and Social Sciences.

References

Duara, P. (2004). Decolonization: Perspectives from Now and Then. London: Routledge.

Foucault, M. (1975). Discipline and Punish. London: Tavistock.

Foucault, M. (1980). The politics of health in the eighteenth century. In Power/knowledge, Selected Interviews and Other Writings 1972-1977, ed. C. Gordon: Brighton: Harvester Press.

Fox, N. J. (1993). Postmodernism, Sociology and Health. Buckingham: Open University Press.

Gunaratne, S. A. (1999). The Media in Asia: An Overview. *Gazette (Leiden, Netherlands)* *61*(3–4), 197–223. https://doi.org/10.1177/0016549299061003002

International Commission of Jurists. (2014, September 4). Malaysia: ICJ condemns the use of sedition to suppress freedom of expression, calls for the abolition of the Sedition Act. https://www.icj.org/malaysia-icj-condemns-the-use-of-sedition-to-suppress-freedom-of-expression-calls-for-the-abolition-of-the-sedition-act/

Lyons, L., & Gomez, J. (2005). Moving beyond the OB Markers: Rethinking the Space of Civil Society in Singapore. *Sojourn: Journal of Social Issues in Southeast Asia* *20*(2), 119–131. https://www.muse.jhu.edu/article/400314

Robards, B., & Lincoln, S. (2017). Uncovering Longitudinal Life Narratives: Scrolling Back on Facebook. *Qualitative Research 17*(6), 715–730. https://doi.org/10.1177/1468794117700707

Williams, R., & Edge, D. (1996). The Social Shaping of Technology. *Research Policy 25*, 856–899. https://doi.org/10.1016/0048-7333(96)00885-2

1 Exploring Methodological Issues in Studying Contentious Communication on Malaysian Social Media

Pauline Pooi Yin Leong

Introduction

Digital media emerged in Malaysia as a result of the government's initiative to tap into the information and communications technology. The Malaysian government created the Multimedia Super Corridor in 1996 to lure world-class multinational technology companies into the country to boost its local knowledge economy (Leong, 2019). While this initiative enabled Malaysia to enter the digital economy, it also set off a chain of events that had a far-reaching impact on the country's political and democratic process. Digital media enabled the opposition and civil society to circumvent the government's monopoly of traditional media and provided the medium for Malaysians to obtain information that differed from the official narrative (Leong, 2019). From listservs to usenet groups, websites, blogs, and social media, each digital iteration enhanced political competition by transforming the public sphere for netizens to discuss socio-political issues that shape narratives and influence public discourse, thus catalysing political change.

It is in this context that many scholars conduct research on Malaysia's cyberspace, which reflects its multi-cultural polyglot population consisting of *bumiputeras* (Malays and Indigenous natives), Chinese, and Indians who speak the national language Bahasa Malaysia, English, Mandarin, and Tamil as well as other dialects. Thus, the myriad Malaysian cyberspace consists of many different online communities existing across various social media platforms, each with its own subculture, characteristics, and agenda. This makes cyberspace an interesting setting for academic research as there are many facets to be explored. However, conducting internet research in Malaysia can be challenging, given the fragmented nature of the Malaysian digital space that encompasses many different parallel online communities, each with its own language, culture, and raison d'être. Therefore, studies that comprehensively assess the overall online public sentiment and reactions require proper planning and focus. The purpose of this chapter is to examine some methodological issues faced by Malaysian researchers while investigating contentious communication on social media, which has not been comprehensively

DOI: 10.4324/9781003619369-2

researched on and discussed in the review of literature. The author aims to do so by discussing her experience in planning and executing two small-scaled research projects that she had embarked on previously – one on the perception and acceptance of online satire among youths in Malaysia, and the other on trolling and hate speech among user-generated comments in an online news portal.

Framework of the Research Process

There are two approaches that guide the research process: Ontology, which is the study of "being" and concerned with the nature of existence and structure of reality (Crotty, 1998), and epistemology, which is the assumption made about the kind or nature of knowledge (Richards et al., 2003). Researchers also select the theoretical paradigms that underpin their research such as positivism which focuses on objectivity and evidence in searching for truth and reality; subjectivism which believes that reality or truth is based on the perceptions and meanings ascribed to the object(s) by the subjects under investigation (Saunders et al., 2009); and constructivism or interpretivism where meaning or truth emerges from interactions between the subject and object (Crotty, 1998). The theoretical paradigm provides strong scientific foundation to develop the study's methodology and methods (Lederman & Lederman, 2015), which grounds the logic, criteria and context for the methodology (Crotty, 1998).

Researching Contentious Communication in Malaysia

In Malaysia, the right to free speech and expression is enshrined in Article 10(1)(a) of the Malaysian Federal Constitution but limitations to this fundamental liberty can be found in Article 10(2)(a), which allows Parliament to enact legislation that restricts free speech on eight grounds, including public order (Federal Constitution of Malaysia, 1957). These legislations include the Sedition Act, the Communications and Multimedia Act, and the Penal Code which regulate speech that is "acceptable" or "out of bounds" (Human Rights Watch, 2021). In authoritarian systems such as Malaysia, the government is often concerned about "contentious journalism" whereby internet-based alternative media are able to challenge the normative consensus in the public sphere (George, 2006). Thus, there is less tolerance towards contentious speech such as political satire that challenges the status quo and a dominant narrative that exists in the public sphere (Loh, 2021).

Political satire is a part of civic discourse in Malaysia (Liang, 2020), but its understanding and acceptance as part of free speech is often contentious because it mocks the political process and actors, and criticises those who walk the corridors of power (Chen, 2016). Prior to the emergence of internet and social media, political humour and satire that comment on socio-political issues of the day appeared mainly in Malay humour magazines and newspapers from the late-70s into the early-80s (Provencher, 1990). The subsequent rise of digital media enabled the appearance of "citizen satire" to describe satirical and humorous content that is created and circulated by individual netizens (Higgie, 2015), resulting in user-generated content such as memes becoming viral. Humour and satire are creative strategies used by Malaysians to voice their feelings and reactions to the socio-political issues that they experience in their lives, to sarcastically mock the authorities and political leadership. It provides a space for political discussion and critique and for creators to engage with the community (Philip, 2021). Political cartoonists and satirists such as Zunar and Fahmi Reza also use social media to publicise their works which are wildly popular across different ethnic communities (Griffiths, 2019), but have not been well received by the authorities. Both have been investigated under the Sedition Act for breaching perceived "out of bound" markers-an indicator of the restricted public space for political satire. While there have been judicial cases that discuss the limit of satire in Malaysia, there has been minimal research conducted on the understanding of this concept among its citizens.

The Malaysian government is also concerned about hate speech affecting inter-ethnic relations due to its past history of racial riots in 1969, which resulted in deaths. Several factors led to this incident, including the post-independence rift between Malays and non-Malays regarding social and political developments (Kua, 2007), the issue of the special position of Malays, and racial insults that occurred post-elections (Comber, 1983). Although the country has not experienced such violence since then, there is still simmering tension under the surface when it comes to matters of race and religion. A 2011 survey conducted by opinion research firm Merdeka Centre found that different ethnic groups in Malaysia still experienced feelings of misunderstanding, apprehension, and distrust (Merdeka Centre, 2011). While Malays believe that it is important to recognise their historical position, non-Malays are dissatisfied with the former's privileges under the government's affirmative action policies post-1969, which the latter perceives to be biased and unfair (Devichand, 2007). Hence, the government polices the cyber-environment in an effort to maintain public order through a legislative restriction, which has resulted in a "chilling effect" and self-censorship among netizens who want to avoid being hauled up by the authorities (Human Rights Watch, 2015).

It is in this context that two research projects were conducted to examine contentious communication in Malaysia: The first is political satire and the second is hate speech and trolling. In the first study, researchers decided to examine the perception and acceptance of youths about satire in Malaysia in relation to a Bahasa Malaysia parody video that was posted on YouTube by Malaysian radio station BFM (The Straits Times, 2015). While the aim of the video was to highlight the hypocrisy of authorities, it caused an uproar in the Malay-Muslim community as it touched on the issue of religion, resulting in police reports and death threats against the presenter in the video (Boo, 2015). Other ethnic groups, however, did not have the same reaction, which was why the researchers decided to only focus on the Malay-Muslim community due to limitations of time and resources.

The research team based the study on the epistemological approach because the purpose was to examine the subjects' understanding and acceptance of satire. Furthermore, the concept of satire is fluid and dependent on cultural perspectives and knowledge of the Malay-Muslim community when it encounters media content. Hence, the study utilised the theoretical framework of social constructionism because the objective was to discover meaning and truth from the perspective of subjects under investigation who were exposed to the online satire video. In social constructivism, individuals develop subjective meanings based on their experiences towards certain objects or things which are varied and manifold. Thus, the purpose of such research is to investigate the complexity of views among participants (Creswell & Poth, 2018). Based on the research approach and theoretical framework, the research team decided to collect data through focus group discussions, which is the appropriate research methodology because new useful in-depth information can emerge from conversations between the respondents as they build on each other's comments and personal experiences, thus enabling researchers to examine the complexity of views (Krueger & Casey, 2015). Each respondent's comment may stimulate others to pursue new lines of discussion, and the snowball effect will result in multiplicity of views which is the aim of social constructionism.

The second study on hate speech and trolling examined comments in online news reports that were published in Bahasa Malaysia, English, and Chinese by news portal *Malaysiakini* about a racial brawl that occurred following an incident at a Kuala Lumpur mall selling electronic products (Malaysiakini, 2015). The purpose of the study was to investigate the extent of hate speech and trolling on the internet among Malaysian netizens given that they are operating in a restrictive environment with regard to free speech. Trolling is a part of internet culture where users intentionally post provocative or offensive messages to elicit attention, for personal amusement or out of boredom (Vincente, 2020). Malaysian netizens often troll their political leaders as a form of humour and sarcasm (Raja Nur Afiqah et al., 2018) in avenues such as Facebook page *Tentera Troll Kebangsaan Malaysia* (TTKM, National Troll Army) (Tentera Troll Kebangsaan Malaysia - Reloaded, 2021) and Malaysia's version of *The Onion – The Tapir Times* (The Tapir Times, 2021). In an interview with online news portal *Malaysiakini*, TTKM said that its trolling posts are satirical critiques of Malaysia's political environment to counter propaganda by political cybertroopers. It believes it is continuing a tradition of Malay popular culture that has existed for decades (Lee & Kerr, 2020). TTKM's trolling is also part of its objective of political education to encourage youths to think critically about politics and politicians (Ainaa, 2019).

However, this is often viewed negatively by authorities and establishment such as Federal Territories Mufti Datuk Seri Zulkifli Mohamad Al-Bakri, who warned that trolling violates the Syariah code and "can only lead to seditious statements, spreading of lies and inciting hatred" (Prakash, 2018). While there have been studies examining hate speech and trolling in general (Lee & Kerr, 2020; Mohd Azizuddin et al., 2016; Murni & Shahir, 2014; Raja Nur Afiqah et al., 2018), there has been minimal studies done to examine the extent to which these concepts exist in user-generated comments, especially among the three main language groups in Malaysia. In this study, the team approached this research from the ontological perspective which is about the nature of reality and its characteristics (Creswell & Poth, 2018). As such, the study of hate speech was informed by the way it was defined by the legislative framework in Malaysia. The researchers positioned their research on the theoretical philosophy of positivism and objectivity, which meant that the team decided to employ quantitative methodology to deductively examine the research objective, and utilised content analysis as a method to collect, analyse, and interpret the data, which were the user-generated comments below the Malaysiakini articles in Bahasa Malaysia, English, and Chinese on the racial riot.

Methodological Issues in the Research Process

Cultural and Language Competencies of the Research Team

During the process of collecting and analysing the data, the research teams encountered methodological issues, specifically in areas of cultural and language competency, given that the Malaysian population under investigation is from diverse ethnic, cultural, and religious groups as well as socio-economic classes. In the first study on the perception and acceptance of online satire among youths in Malaysia, the research team was cognisant of the importance of having a suitable person to facilitate the focus group discussions so that rich and appropriate data can be extracted from participants' conversation. Reflexivity is the awareness that the researcher and object of study affect each other mutually and continually in the research process. There are two key elements: Interpretation, which is acceptance that the research process is influenced by the researchers' assumptions based on the positionality of their values, language, culture, and background; and reflection, where researchers contemplate on how their perceptions, theories, ideology, and cultural assumptions inform the interpretation (Alvesson & Skoldburg, 2000). The qualitative, subjective nature of such research means that researchers, through reflexivity, recognise how their identity and contextual positionality augment the construction of the research process (Swaminathan & Mulvihill, 2018).

The research team, which consisted of two Malaysian Chinese (including the author) and one Malaysian Malay-Muslim, decided to appoint the latter to facilitate the focus group discussions as she was an insider in the community under investigation, being of the same ethnic group and religious orientation of the participants who were Malaysian undergraduates from a local Islamic university. The sessions were conducted in Bahasa Malaysia, which is the national language and mother tongue of the facilitator and participants. The Insider Doctrine asserted that insider researchers were in a unique position to comprehend the lived experiences of groups in which they were members of (Merton, 1972), and the shared identity, language, and experience with research participants (Asselin, 2003) gave researchers some legitimacy (Adler & Adler, 1987). There are three main advantages of being an insider. Firstly, the researcher has a keen understanding of the group's culture (Bonner & Tolhurst, 2002); secondly, the natural ability to interact with group members; and lastly, greater relational intimacy due to shared culture and beliefs (Bonner & Tolhurst, 2002). The insider status is the starting point for researchers to lay the foundation for trust and openness which builds rapport and confidence among the respondents who are likely to be more willing to share their views and stories, thus providing richer data for the study (Berger, 2013; Dwyer & Buckle, 2009). However, there is a risk that the researcher's overfamiliarity with the research topic and/or participants could limit objectivity; the researcher might end up making inadvertent erroneous assumptions and bias based on previous personal knowledge and/or experience (DeLyser, 2001; Gerrish, 1997; Hewitt-Taylor, 2002). Insiders may also struggle to balance their role as a group member which requires developing rapport with participants, and as a researcher which requires maintaining distance for objective data analysis (Breen, 2007). Outsiders, on the other hand, are seen to be more objective and critical (Hellawell, 2006) and are able to review the group dynamics and assumptions in the discourse as external experts (Dwyer & Buckle, 2009). Thus, research teams consisting of insiders and outsiders would have the advantages of both positionalities while minimising the disadvantages (Pugh et al., 2000). Hence, the research team had two other members who were ethnic Chinese and outsiders to the Malay-Muslim focus group participants; the formers' positions ensured that there was adequate distance to observe and analyse the data collection to reduce bias and possible presumptions. They observed their team member's facilitation of the focus groups and provided feedback after each session so as to improve the data collection process.

However, in reality, researchers are never completely insiders or outsiders as their identities are relative, depending on the participants' characteristics with respect to the researchers as well as the research topic and situation (Mercer, 2007). Instead of the strict insider/outsider dichotomy, Dwyer and Buckle (2009) proposed "the space between" framework which posits that researchers are not completely insiders nor outsiders; they occupy different spaces depending on the context of the research project. The "space between" is multidimensional where the researchers' identities and culture influence their position in the research project, and they have the responsibility to understand their position and how it might affect the research process and outcomes (Serrant-Green, 2002). According to Banks (1998), the differences in researchers' knowledge and values within their ethnic and cultural communities has given rise to four categories of positionality – Indigenous-insider, Indigenous-outsider, external-insider, and external-outsider-which are mediated by their characteristics such as gender, class, religion, and age. Thus, although the Malay-Muslim focus group facilitator is an Indigenous member, her status would be that of the Indigenous-outsider as she is of a different age group from the participants; while the other Chinese researchers are external-insiders because they are conversant in Bahasa Malaysia, the language of the participants, although they are not from the same ethnic community. Hence, the combined positionalities of the researchers enabled appropriate data collection for analysis.

Reflexivity on the research team's positionality is important as it affects participant recruitment as well as data analysis. In the study on satire, there was little difficulty in recruiting Malay-Muslim undergraduates as they were of the same ethnicity and religion as the Malay-Muslim researcher, as well as in the same university. However, the ethnic Chinese researchers had a harder time recruiting Malay-Muslim adult participants as their network within the community was not sufficiently strong. Despite sending the focus group invitations to their Malay-Muslim friends and contacts, the ethnic Chinese researchers were unable to recruit sufficient respondents. They had to conduct a second round of recruitment by asking their Chinese and Indian friends and contacts to circulate the invitation to the latter's Malay-Muslim network, which finally enabled the team to obtain sufficient respondents for the focus group.

In the study on trolling and hate speech, the research team's positionality and language competencies affected the research process during data analysis. While all three researchers were able to understand and interpret the user-generated comments in English, only two were able to understand Bahasa Malaysia, and one was fluent in Chinese, which meant that the latter's role was to analyse the Chinese comments. In the case of the Bahasa Malaysia comments, two researchers were able to analyse most of the data as they were conversant in the language. However, they encountered some difficulties in understanding the abbreviations and colloquialisms in a few comments as they were Indigenous outsiders who were unfamiliar with the cultural nuances and lingo that were used. For example, the Malay word "*balun*" means to beat or thrash someone, but it is colloquially used to describe someone eating food ravenously. The Malaysian researchers resorted to asking friends who are insiders in the Malay-Muslim community to explain the meaning behind some of the Bahasa Malaysia colloquial comments. The research team did not face any issues in analysing English and Chinese comments as they were insiders and understood the abbreviations and informal use of various terms. It is clear that reflexivity of the team's positionality, especially composition of insider members of the community subject under investigation, is essential to the successful design and execution of the research project.

Analytical Frameworks for Categorising Data

In the study on trolling and hate speech, the researchers encountered difficulty during the data analysis stage while attempting to categorise the content in online comments. This is because definitions of hate speech vary among different societies, depending on their history and level of tolerance, with developed countries taking a more "relaxed" approached compared to developing countries (Iyer, 2010). Scholars have been unable to agree on a globally accepted understanding of hate speech that differentiates between speech that should legally be restricted vis-à-vis unpleasant speech that should be allowed (George, 2016). However, they agree that hate speech harms society through identifying a group or its representatives by their characteristics such as race, religion, and/or sexual orientation and communicating extremely negative ideas about them (Waltman & Hass, 2011). In Malaysia, there are several laws that govern the realm of hate speech, chief of which is the Sedition Act. While English common law on sedition adopts a liberal approach to allow robust criticism and only criminalising extreme speech, the Sedition Act in Malaysia criminalises any speech that has a "seditious tendency" which is likely to "bring into hatred or contempt or to excite disaffection against any ruler" or "to promote feelings of ill will, hostility or hatred" between different groups on the basis of race, class, or religion (Jeyaseelen, 2009). The Sedition Act has also been criticised for suppressing legitimate criticisms against authorities, which complicates the analysis of hate speech in the study as the Malaysian framework for hate speech differs somewhat from the general international standards. The researchers found difficulty in categorising the comments which might be considered as legitimate speech based on the international definitions but may breach the Malaysian legislative framework. In the case of trolling, although there are definitions and characteristics that classify them (Phillips, 2015), identifying trolls in the Malaysia context requires deeper understanding of the sub-text and sub-culture among the different language groups.

Lastly, the researchers discovered that there were, in fact, minimal hate speech comments and trolling. At most, there were criticisms that were legitimately allowed under Malaysian law. The research team then realised that the comments are likely to have been moderated by Malaysiakini's editorial team due to legal constraints and fear of authorities taking action to stop its operations, if it allowed the publication of user-generated content that breached out-of-bound markers. It is also possible that self-censorship occurs as the public is aware of the heavy penalties that they face if they breach any of the laws that regulate free speech. This means that the data obtained have been "sanitised" and may not be reflective of the actual public opinion of Malaysian netizens.

Conclusion

In summary, there are many considerations in the research process when studying contentious communication on Malaysian social media, especially in relation to the project's methodology and design, as well as composition of team members. Researchers need to be aware of the socio-political and legal environment when initiating and planning research projects to study contentious communication in Malaysia. For example, in the study on trolling and hate speech, legal constraints caused a chilling effect on media portals and netizens which affected the quality of data in cyberspace, because user-generated comments on the internet may be moderated and do not necessarily reflect the reality of public opinion on issues in Malaysia. Proper research design in the initial stages could have anticipated and avoided such limitations. For example, if the aim is to examine public sentiment, instead of conducting content analysis of online content, researchers can administer an anonymous multi-lingual survey that encompasses a larger segment of the population or conduct focus groups, so that they are able to gather pertinent and useful data that would fulfil their research objectives. Alternatively, researchers can identify other public forums which are less moderated or unmoderated, and engage big data analytical software to examine the comments in various online platforms.

The reflexivity of the research team's positionality is also important when conducting any study using traditional qualitative approaches such as focus groups and interviews in Malaysia, due to its pluralistic society with diverse ethnicities, cultures, languages, and religions. It is important that the research team comprises members who have the necessary expertise and skillsets such as language and cultural competencies so as to be able to access the population under investigation, as the quality of data is dependent on the participation of appropriate respondents. Composition of research team members should consist of insiders who can facilitate the recruitment of suitable participants, as well as assist in analysing data emerging from the discourse among the different communities with varied cultures, language, and faith practices. The team should also include outsiders who would be able to provide objective expert perspectives on the research methodology and design. If the study requires the understanding of special concepts or linguistic skills, the inclusion of subject matter experts in the research team can contribute to more comprehensive data analysis. Thus, proper planning of the research design and composition of research team members from the

14   *Internet Popular Culture and (Everyday) Politics*

initial stages are important to ensure the successful execution and completion of research projects in Malaysia.

References

Adler, P. A., & Adler, P. (1987). Membership Roles in Field Research. Thousand Oaks, CA: Sage.

Ainaa, A. (2019, 10 February). 'Troll army' aims to raise political awareness in young voters. Free Malaysia Today. https://www.freemalaysiatoday.com/category/nation/2019/02/10/troll-army-aims-to-raise-political-awareness-in-young-voters/

Alvesson, M., & Skoldburg, K. (2000). Reflexive Methodology: New Vistas for Qualitative Research. London: Sage.

Asselin, M. E. (2003). Insider Research: Issues to Consider When Doing Qualitative Research in Your Own Setting. *Journal for Nurses in Staff Development 19*(2), 99–103.

Banks, J. A. (1998). The Lives and Values of Researchers: Implications for Educating Citizens in a Multicultural Society. *Educational Researcher 27*(7), 4–17.

Berger, R. (2013). Now I See It, Now I Don't: Researcher's Position and Reflexivity in Qualitative Research. *Qualitative Research 15*(2), 219–234. https://doi.org/10.1177/1468794112468475

Bonner, A., & Tolhurst, G. (2002). Insider-Outsider Perspectives of Participant Observation. *Nurse Researcher 9*(4), 7–19.

Boo, S. -L. (2015, 20 March). BFM journalist gets death, rape threats over video questioning hudud. Malay Mail. https://www.malaymail.com/news/malaysia/2015/03/20/bfm-journalist-gets-death-rape-threats-over-video-questioning-hudud/863097

Breen, L. J. (2007). The Researcher 'in the Middle': Negotiating the Insider/Outsider Dichotomy. *The Australian Community Psychologist 19*(1), 163–174. https://psychology.org.au/aps/media/acp/breen_19(1).pdf

Chen, K. W. (2016). Citizen satire in Malaysia and Singapore: Why and how socio-political humour communicates dissent on Facebook University of Canterbury]. New Zealand. https://ir.canterbury.ac.nz/handle/10092/12794

Comber, L. (1983). 13 May 1963: A Historical Survey of Sino-Malay Relations. Singapore: Heinemann Educational Books (Asia) Ltd.

Creswell, J. W., & Poth, C. N. (2018). Qualitative Inquiry and Research Design: Choosing Among Five Approaches (4th ed.). Thousand Oaks, CA: SAGE Publications, Inc.

Crotty, M. (1998). The Foundations of Social Research: Meaning and Perspective in the Research Process (1st ed.). London: SAGE Publications.

DeLyser, D. (2001). "Do You Really Live Here?" Thoughts on Insider Research. *The Geographical Review 91*(1/2, Doing Fieldwork (Jan-Apr)), 441–453.

Devichand, A. (2007, 8 November). Racial tensions simmer in Malaysia. Al-Jazeera https://www.aljazeera.com/news/2007/11/8/racial-tensions-simmer-in-malaysia

Dwyer, S. C., & Buckle, J. L. (2009). The Space Between: On Being an Insider-Outsider in Qualitative Research. *International Journal of Qualitative Methods 8*(1), 54–63. https://doi.org/10.1177/160940690900800105

Federal Constitution of Malaysia (1957). [16th reprint on 15 October 2020]. https://lom.agc.gov.my/federal-constitution.php

George, C. (2006). Contentious Journalism and the Internet: Towards Democratic Discourse in Malaysia and Singapore. Singapore: Singapore University Press, NUS Publishing.

George, C. (2016). Hate Spin as Politics by Other Means. In Hate Spin: The Manufacture of Religious Offense and Its Threat to Democracy (pp. 1–23). Cambridge, MA: MIT Press.

Gerrish, K. (1997). Being a 'Marginal Native': Dilemmas of the Participant Observer. *Nurse Researcher 5*(1), 25–34.

Griffiths, J. (2019, 29 May). The cartoonists who helped take down a Malaysian prime minister. Cable News Network. https://edition.cnn.com/style/article/malaysia-1mdb-najib-zunar-fahmi-reza-intl/index.html

Hellawell, D. (2006). Analysis of the Insider-Outsider Concept as a Heuristic Device to Develop Reflexivity in Students Doing Qualitative Research. *Inside-out: Teaching in Higher Education 11*(4), 483–494. https://doi.org/10.1080/13562510600874292

Hewitt-Taylor, J. (2002). Insider Knowledge: Issues in Insider Research. *Nursing Standard 16*(46), 33–35.

Higgie, R. (2015). The Satirists Formerly Known as the Audience: Citizen Satire, Global Landscapes and the Reorientation of Political Debate. In J. Q. Hartley (Ed.), Re-Orientation: Trans-Cultural, Trans-Lingual and Trans-Media Studies in Narrative, Language, Identity and Knowledge (pp. 161–178). Shanghai: Fudan University Press. https://static1.squarespace.com/static/5ea65d5f97297049a869ba34/t/5eafb1a26468d57b5ba89328/1588572598294/The±Satirists±Formerly±Known±as±the±Audience.pdf

Human Rights Watch. (2015). Creating a culture of fear: The criminalization of peaceful expression in Malaysia. https://www.hrw.org/report/2015/10/27/creating-culture-fear/criminalization-peaceful-expression-malaysia

Human Rights Watch. (2021). Malaysia: Free speech under increasing threat. Human Rights Watch. Retrieved 7 December 2021 from https://www.hrw.org/news/2021/05/19/malaysia-free-speech-under-increasing-threat

Iyer, V. (2010). Media Coverage of Sensitive Matters. In Media Law Handbook. Kuala Lumpur: Asia-Pacific Institute for Broadcasting Development (AIBD).

Jeyaseelen, A. (2009). Seditious Tendency? Politcal Patronisation of Free Speech and Expression in Malaysia. Malaysia: Education and Research Association (ERA) for Consumers.

Krueger, R. A., & Casey, M. A. (2015). Focus Groups: A Practical Guide for Applied Research (5th ed.). Thousand Oaks, CA: SAGE Publications, Inc.

Kua, K. S. (2007). 13 May: Declassified Documents on the Malaysia Riots of 1969. Malaysia: Suaram Komunikasi.

Lederman, N. G., & Lederman, J. S. (2015). What Is a Theoretical Framework? A Practical Answer. *Journal of Science Teacher Education 26*, 593–597.

Lee, C. A. L., & Kerr, E. (2020). Trolls at the Polls. *First Monday 25*(6 (1 June 2020)). https://doi.org/10.5210/fm.v25i6.10704

Leong, P. P. Y. (2019). Introduction. In Malaysian Politics in the New Media Age: Implications on the Political Communication Process (pp. 4–7). Singapore: Springer Nature. https://doi.org/10.1007/978-981-13-8783-8

Liang, I. H. (2020, 27 April). Of satire, parody and fake news. Malaysian Public Law. Retrieved 3 December from https://malaysianpubliclaw.com/of-satire-parody-and-fake-news/

Loh, B. Y. (2021, 15 April). In defence of political satire. Malaysiakini. https://www.malaysiakini.com/columns/570748

Malaysiakini. (2015, 12 July). Shop workers beaten in Low Yat Plaza scuffle. Malaysiakini. https://www.malaysiakini.com/news/304871

Mercer, J. (2007). The Challenges of Insider Research in Educational Institutions: Wielding a Double-Edged Sword and Resolving Delicate Dilemmas. Oxford Review of Education, 33, 1–17.

Merdeka Centre. (2011, 12 August). Public confidence in state of ethnic relations decline. https://www.merdeka.org/v4/phocadownload/News/2011%20ethnic%20relations%20poll%20news%20release%20-%20final.pdf

Merton, R. (1972). Insiders and Outsiders: A Chapter in the Sociology of Knowledge. *American Journal of Sociology 78*(July), 9–47. https://www.d.umn.edu/cla/faculty/jhamlin/4111/Readings/MertonKnowledge.pdf

Mohd Azizuddin, M. S., Muhammad Zaki, A., & Ratnaria, W. (2016). Freedom of the Internet in Malaysia. *The Social Sciences 11*(7), 1343–1349.

Murni, W. M. N., & Shahir, A. R. (2014). Regulating Hate Speech on Social Media: Should We or Shouldn't We? *Malayan Law Journal 4*, cxxix.

Philip, S. (2021). Satire and Community in the Time of COVID-19: An Analysis of Ernest Ng's Covidball Z. *Journal of Postcolonial Writing 57*(5), 709–722. https://doi.org/10.1080/17449855.2021.1982114

Phillips, W. (2015). This Is Why We Can't Have Nice Things: Mapping the Relationship between Online Trolling and Mainstream Culture. Cambridge, MA: The MIT Press.

Prakash, G. (2018). FT mufti advises Muslims not to troll others, says unIslamic. Malay Mail. https://www.malaymail.com/news/malaysia/2018/12/28/ft-mufti-advises-muslims-not-to-troll-others-says-unislamic/1707145

Provencher, R. (1990). Covering Malay Humor Magazines: Satire and Parody of Malaysian Political Dilemmas. *Crossroads: An Interdisciplinary Journal of Southeast Asian Studies 5*(2), 1–25. https://www.jstor.org/stable/40860308

Pugh, J., Mitchell, M., & Brooks, F. (2000). Insider/Outsider Partnerships in an Ethnographic Study of Shared Governance. *Nursing Standard 27*, 43–44.

Raja Nur Afiqah, R. Z., Noor Sulastry Yurni, A., Mohd Azizuddin, M. S., & Haslina, M. (2018). Satira politik: Analisis internet trolling di Malaysia (Political Satire: Analysis on Internet Trolling in Malaysia). *Jurnal Komunikasi/ Malaysian Journal of Communication 34*(2), 223–242. http://doi.org/10.17576/JKMJC-2018-3402-14

Richards, K. (2003). Qualitative Inquiry in TESOL. Houndmills, Basingstoke, Hampshire and New York, NY: Palgrave Macmillan

Saunders, M., Lewis, P., & Thornhill, A. (2009). Research Methods for Business Students (5th ed.). Edinburgh, Harlow, Essex, England: Pearson Education Limited.

Serrant-Green, L. (2002). Black on Black: Methodological Issues for Black Researchers Working in Minority Ethnic Communities. *Nurse Researcher 9*(4), 30–44.

Swaminathan, R., & Mulvihill, T. M. (2018). Teaching Qualitative Research: Strategies for Engaging Emerging Scholars. New York, NY: Guildford Press.

Tentera Troll Kebangsaan Malaysia - Reloaded. (2021). https://www.facebook.com/TTKMRELOADED/

The Straits Times. (2015, 20 March). Malaysia's radio station removes hudud video after presenter threatened. The Straits Times. https://www.straitstimes.com/asia/se-asia/malaysias-radio-station-removes-hudud-video-after-presenter-threatened

The Tapir Times [@thetapirtimes]. (2021). https://www.facebook.com/thetapirtimes/

Vincente, V. (2020, 21 January). What is an internet troll? (and how to handle trolls). How-To Geek. https://www.howtogeek.com/465416/what-is-an-internet-troll-and-how-to-handle-trolls/

Waltman, M., & Hass, J. (2011). The Communication of Hate. New York, NY: Peter Lang.

2 Social Media-Circulated Underground Music and Politics

The Case of the *Lamidet* Society

Muria Endah Sokowati and Fajar Junaedi

Introduction

The story of the underground scene in Indonesia reflects the struggle of youth to enter a more democratic era in the face of decades of dictatorship towards greater democracy (Wallach, 2005). President Suharto ran a dictatorship from 1966 to the late 1990s. In May 1998, Suharto's authority finally ended when he stepped down in response to the mass demonstrations conducted by students and activists, marking, the beginning of a more democratic era. Wallach (2005) argued that the development of the underground music scene reflects the emergence of democracy, specifically from the 1990s to the period after 1998. Most of the mass demonstration participants who dramatically overthrew Suharto's autocratic regime were underground musicians and fans (Wallach, 2005), gathered in big cities like Jakarta, Bandung, and Yogyakarta. They vigorously criticised Suharto's government and global capitalism, sometimes using Satanic themes in their song titles, lyrics, album covers, performances, and merchandise (Pickles, 2000; Wallach, 2008).

In the post-New Order period (during the 2000s), underground music has been critical of Indonesian politics (Wallach, 2003). Young people in Indonesia increasingly have the courage to express their disagreement on socio-political issues, for example, the dispassionate state policies that are employed when dealing with marginalised groups in land eviction cases. Thus, underground music remains important roles in shaping the culture of democracy in Indonesia.

Quoting Wallach (2005), most successful underground bands produced songs and distinctive styles that address their fears, emotions, and aspirations. The musicians and fans are more comfortable with the homegrown sound because it better addresses their concerns and aspirations. Song themes are also localised. Baulch (2003), for example, argued that some underground metal communities become the medium for articulating their resistance to the development and management of Balinese tourist sites by investors from Jakarta.

DOI: 10.4324/9781003619369-3

Inspired by Baulch's study, we are interested in observing how the underground scene has incorporated local issues and problems into the music and lyrics. We explored underground music with a local theme in the *Lamidet* Society, a group of young people who play underground music and have concerns about urban issues in Yogyakarta. Their concerns for urban problems are reflected in their songs, musical performances, zines, and merchandise.

Based on his research on a metal band in Bandung, Wallach (2003, p. 61) argued that the underground music community are usually not politically active because they do not always connect their music to broader social or political issues. It is, however, different in the case of the *Lamidet* Society, which uses music to protest local government policies.

Formed in 2018, the *Lamidet* Society is a group of young musical artists across genres (punk, metal, and hip-hop) formed because of the shared interest of its members in developing the underground music scene in Yogyakarta. It is also a community based on supporters of *Persatuan Sepak bola Indonesia Mataram* (PSIM), a professional football club in Yogyakarta. The community members come from various backgrounds, ranging from jobless people to online motorcycle taxi drivers, hotel employees, students, and others. Despite their diverse backgrounds, they share the same passion and concern about problems in Yogyakarta, and agreed to play music to express their opinions on the problem. Over time, they have also been bound by a common interest, football. Hence, we see the *Lamidet* Society as a scene, a young community borne of its desire to create values and express its identities through musical practices (Shank, 1994).

The *Lamidet's* members construct their identities as excluded residents due to discriminatory policies. They have been involved in the struggle against the local government using social media and participating in mass demonstrations. Through our research, we learned that interplays between the underground scene, football fandom, and cultural politics have shifted the roles and functions of underground music. Music here is not only the people's tool for expressing their concerns and aspirations, but also functions as an instrument of the *Lamidet* society's political actions, such as joining and initiating mass demonstrations and voicing urban problems in social media.

The *Lamidet* Society consists of supporters of the local football clubs. Their identity as working-class, urban, and marginalised is constructed through their bonds as football fans, and their musical performances and mass demonstrations have included their identity as part of the football fandom. Moreover, the *Lamidet* members' use of the internet as a tool in their struggle is significant. Scholars claim that the internet enables users to actively participate in public issues. It allows users to voice their thoughts (Mitra and Watts, 2002). Jenkins' (2006) concept of participatory culture and Lim's (2003) idea of the internet as a social medium for civil society are examples of internet's ability to empower its users. Similarly, the *Lamidet* Society has also used the internet, specifically social media, to protest and fight against the local administration.

Method

Based on the background of the study, the following questions have guided our research and analysis:

1 How does the use of social media by the *Lamidet* Society relate to its underground music performances?
2 With reference to both of these activities, how does its expression of political critiques relate to its community advocacy?

We conducted several in-depth interviews with members of the *Lamidet* Society. We also initiated a focus group to discuss their experience in circulating their music and social criticism. Simultaneously, additional analysis of their online activities on social media provided further context in which to view how members of the *Lamidet* Society use social media in their struggle. We conducted online observations to collect discussion data on their social media accounts from Twitter, Instagram, and YouTube.

Lamidet Society: A New Generation of the Underground Scene in Yogyakarta

Underground Scene in Yogyakarta

Based on our interview of Adnan Kusuma, a member of a local punk band, the underground scene in Yogyakarta and its concerns about the political situation during the New Order started during the 1990s (interview, 6 April 2021). Their expressions and criticisms of the political situation continued after Suharto's resignation. The same concern and critical tradition of social change have also been found in underground music in Yogyakarta. These reflections align with observations by Richter (2012, p. 3), who argued that politically oppositional music gained increasing momentum in the late New Order period to the early 2000s.

Young people's limited access to economic resources and the strong, entrenched position of the music industry made it difficult to produce and organise events. However, this changed when a do it yourself (DIY) spirit grew among young people. They started to create zines and distributed them in photocopy kiosks, raising young people's awareness. The political climate in the 1990s encouraged the strengthening of the DIY culture among young people, leading to greater awareness of creating music, organising, and distributing it. Kusuma mentioned that underground artists produced music by recording it in rented music studios. They also organised concert events in venues such as university campuses, high-school musical stages, urban-village auditoriums, small venues in the city centre, or cafes. Interestingly, artists passed on and publicised their music as files in folders available at warnet (*warung Internet*/Internet cafes), allowing patrons to copy and share music freely. This was perhaps the earliest form of peer-to-peer music sharing, predating the internet.

The fast growth of the internet and communication technology has changed the distribution of underground music. Underground communities later used music provider sites, such as Soundcloud or Reverbnation.com; or music streaming applications, such as JOOX and Spotify. YouTube is also an important platform for distributing music videos. Social media, such as Instagram or Twitter, have become a means to promote the latest works, including marketing various merchandise, such as CDs, T-shirts, and zines.

Criticisms of Urban Development

Yogyakarta is the capital of the Yogyakarta province in Indonesia and has the privileged status of being called the Special Region of Yogyakarta. Its specialty is being the only province that still runs the Monarchy system in Indonesia. Before Indonesia's independence, Yogyakarta had a Sultanate government. At that time, Sri Sultan Hamengku Buwono X became the ruler of Yogyakarta. Thus, based on Law No. 13/2012 concerning the Privileges of the Special Region of Yogyakarta, the government in Yogyakarta is the only one running an aristocratic system in which the leader is not elected by the people through democratic elections but based on lineage. The Sultan receives great authority from the central government (Rifayani et al., 2013).

The practice of monarchy within the state has contributed to some serious problems, such as agrarian conflicts. Yogyakarta is a case in point. With much tourism potential because of the many cultural heritage and natural attractions from the mountains to the coast, Yogyakarta has become one of the leading tourist destinations in Indonesia. Consequently, since 2012, new hotels have been constructed and resulted in increasing congestion, loss of public and green spaces, and soaring land prices. Wealthy investors are increasingly controlling strategic spaces in the city centre, while residents are starting to be evicted and forced to move out of the city (Sesanti, 2016).

Underground bands remain critical, especially of the Yogyakarta government. The regional autonomy policy encourages provinces to regulate the development of their respective regions (Laksono et al., 2011). Kusuma explained that their disappointment with the Yogyakarta Government or the Sultan's policy is driven by the many residents who are evicted due to rising land prices. Land in the city is mostly dominated by immigrants and investors (Sesanti, 2016, p. 7).

Interacting with Local Football Supporters

The underground community members' concern about urban problems is energised when they hang out with the *Brajamusti* supporters' group, one of the PSIM supporters. According to Fuller (2014, p. 3), the members of the *Brajamusti* group have been considered troublemakers and outsiders because their behaviour conflicts with acceptable Javanese norms. Since then, *Brajamusti's* members have attempted to change their public image. They identify themselves as Javanese and people of Yogyakarta by upholding the values of respect, loyalty, sincerity, diligence, and tradition. The group consists of a complex network of activists and young people who come from various economic and social backgrounds. Their dedication to *Brajamusti* and PSIM is reflected in their support for Yogyakarta's identity, and their criticism of the city's marginalisation of the urban poor as a result of its rapid growth.

There is an intersection of interest between the underground community and the *Brajamusti*. Kusuma emphasised that many of *Brajamusti's* members and their solid relationships encouraged them to turn their concerns into real political actions. The *Lamidet* Society was then formed, comprising members who are musicians and fans of underground music and *Brajamusti* members.

Musical Performance as the Forefront of Political Actions

Lamidet people originated from the working class, but they tend to identify and organise themselves with the poor instead. This pattern of behaviour aligns with Martin-Iverson's study (2014) of punk communities in Indonesia. Their identification with the poor reflect their concern for the urban poor in Yogyakarta. As underground community members, their concern is manifested through music and stage. They produce and distribute albums that voice their concern and widen the audience, and in doing so, they create platforms for protest.

Music as Protest

In 2012 and 2013, *Lamidet* Society members presented a collective music performance entitled The Underground Conspiracy. It was the first event of their involvement with underground music. In the following years, they organised the next collective music concert called From Terrace to the Stage (FTTS). FTTS was first held in May 2018. It was a community-driven event compared to other music concerts in Yogyakarta. The gig was for people who were fans of underground music and local football. Some bands that performed, such as DOM 65 and Straight Answer, were well-known as fans of PSIM. Political issues had not yet become a concern during this first FTTS. The main focus was on providing a stage for local bands in Yogyakarta, especially those with a theme song about PSIM. In November 2019, FTTS launched the first compilation album entitled *Titik Nol* (Zero Point). The next FTTS in December 2019 followed the album launch. In the second FTTS, the bands brought the urban issues to the stage. The main issue of their concern was the class discrimination between poor locals and wealthy immigrants.

Kusuma stated that the local government of Yogyakarta, as a tourism city, established a policy encouraging more visitors, impacting the local population negatively. For example, the construction of a hotel resulted in the elimination of residential water sources around the hotel (Sesanti, 2016). *Lamidet* members also criticised the low regional minimum wage, the exceptionally high price of land, and how properties were only affordable for wealthy immigrants.

In this event, the *Lamidet* Society members carried banners that read Tourism Kills the City to protest against tourism-oriented development that prioritised large investors and cared little for the common people. The other banner read *Nrimo Ing Pandum Dalam Ketimpangan* (Surrender to the Inequality) as their criticism of the existing problem of class inequality. This concert unexpectedly attracted 2,000 spectators. In May 2021, FTTS launched its second compilation album, Urban Hulk, containing songs about football and social issues. Concerts were well-organised and funded independently through the sale of merchandise. They deliberately rejected the offer of several sponsors to maintain their independence. This strategy allowed musical activities run autonomously and free of interference from powerful individuals over mainstream culture (Wallach, 2008).

The Politics of DIY

Based on previous studies, the practice of DIY among underground bands in Yogyakarta is an attempt to avoid mainstream music produced by the music industry (Lukisworo and Sutopo, 2017; Septian and Hendrastomo, 2019). Lukisworo and Sutopo studied Metal DIY, a metal community in Yogyakarta. This community maintains the practice of DIY to resist metal bands starting to be part of the popular music industry. Septian and Hendrastomo's study of the Indie music fan community in Yogyakarta revealed that their predilection for indie music is driven by the spirit of resistance to mainstream music.

However, the DIY practice among musicians and fans in Yogyakarta de-scribed by these two studies does not represent the DIY practices of other communities. We discovered that instead of constructing their identity to distinguish them from musicians and fans of popular music, DIY for the *Lamidet* members is the key strategy of their resistance against the established political system.

Resistance requires autonomy and independence from record labels and financial sponsorship. Autonomy requires a collective network to launch the process of producing and distributing music. The *Lamidet* Society facilitates the same kind of autonomy to oppose authorities. Communication technology enables such resistance by facilitating the process of producing and dis-tributing their works. This is aligned with Moore's (2013, p. 372), assertion that the internet empowers independent artists and labels to compete with the corporate mainstream. Interestingly, our interviews showed that the *Lamidet* Society does not intend to be a part of the industry. Music for its members is merely a way to be devoted to their passion and express their anxiety over urban problems.

The music production process is managed through Terrace Records, an independent label. In addition to making records for online streaming, they also produce songs on compact discs. Each band pays all the expenses for the recording process. They use social media to promote and Spotify to distribute the songs (From Terrace to the Stage, 2020). They also create videos and pod-casts on YouTube. On their YouTube account, From Terrace to the Stage, with 1.68K subscribers, they upload official music videos (for example, Corner At-tack's video for a song titled *Tourism Kills the City* in 2021), live performance footage (for example, Side Kick's performance in 2019 [From Terrace to the Stage, 2019]), and discussions related to urban issues (JITV Pemda DIY, 2018). These accounts also encourage subscriptions to YouTube accounts of bands, such as The Genk, Side Kick, Since KO, and Corner Attack.

The use of these platforms is primarily focused on distributing music to audiences. The bands run collective marketing strategies to support the com-munity. While selling CD albums, merchandise, and zines, there is no legal agreement on the nominal amount of proceeds from sales returned to the band, with each band having a different profit calculation based on the agreement between the band and Terrace Records as the label. Profits gained from the product sale are allocated to organise FTTS. Promotion and sales of these products are carried out through jointly managed social media, such as Twitter and Instagram. The rapid growth of communication technology has facilitated marketing and promoting music quickly and efficiently to broader audiences (Sen, 2010). Social media helps them reach larger audiences, people who pre-viously lived in Yogyakarta or people passionate and concerned about PSIM or football and urban issues. Fans and supporters who come from a wider area can increase product sales. The autonomy of the *Lamidet* Society has become the key means for conducting political actions and will be explained in the following section.

The Political Actions: From Stage to Street

From our research, FTTS is not just a medium for voicing criticism of the inequality in everyday life but also serves as a consolidation of musicians, fans, groups of supporters, and individuals. It is a manifestation of greater political solidarity, which connects to political action. Angger, the chairman of the FTTS committee, explained in an interview with the local media that FTTS is an event where audiences can build friendship networks, and get to know underground music to accommodate similar activities.

Thus, underground music unites groups and individuals with the same interests in the condition of Yogyakarta, which can culminate in street protests. For instance, *Lamidet's* members participated in a mass demonstration against the Law on the Job Creation Act, a law detrimental to workers, in October 2020. The demonstration led to riots, which resulted in destruction of public facilities and arrests. The incident forced them to change their strategy of resistance by using social media.

Social Media as Alternative Mode to Resist

The *Lamidet* Society uses *Lamidet's* accounts on Twitter and Instagram, or accounts belonging to each band, and personal accounts of all community members. @LamidetFM joined Twitter in 2013 and has 1746 followers. It also has two Instagram accounts: @lamidetsociety with 54 posts and 679 followers, and @lamidet_society with 20 posts and 271 followers. They avoid using Facebook because it has heterogeneous users, causes unproductive discussion, and provokes conflicts. Facebook has been seen as tolerant of negative activities, such as stalking, addiction, or invasion of privacy (Stieger, 2019). Aryo, a key person in *Lamidet*, said social media has two functions (Interview, 1 May 2021). First, it allows for sharing of specific topics to attract netizens' attention; second, Twitter is beneficial in mapping the comments of followers, fans, and supporters concerning some issues and is used to recognise followers, fans, and supporters associated with particular topics.

Social media has significantly contributed to producing and distributing critical issues. The content discussed can raise the awareness of its followers and encourage them to speak out. Kusuma emphasised the significant differences before and after 2019 when the *Lamidet* Society actively began to voice urban issues. Followers, fans, and supporters have become more active in speaking out on crucial issues. However, concerns about police surveillance and attacks have also emerged with increased digital footprints.

Fuchs (2016, p. 20) reminded us that social media seems to be supportive of public online activities. Unfortunately, social media does not necessarily take the side of the public in this case. As Kusuma has stated *Lamidet's* social media accounts have been surveilled by local government elites. They make anonymous accounts on Twitter to attack official accounts or other accounts representing the Yogyakarta government, for example, @kratonjogja. Criticising the Yogyakarta government means criticising the sacred institution of the Sultanate. The sultanate institution is recognised by the state as a formal institution, and has been legitimised by the Law No. 13/2012. It strengthens the Sultan's position as leader of tradition, Islamic leader, and also the governor. The Sultan also controls the ownership of land in Yogyakarta. His control over the political, religious, tradition, and economic realms makes the Sultan a sacred figure.

Because it is taboo to criticise the Yogyakarta Sultanate's policy, the *Lamidet* Society has been encouraged to use anonymity, which only applies to personal accounts of the *Lamidet* Society's members. The *Lamidet* Society still uses the real account, @LamidetFm. The incident in October 2020 further solidified their decision to maintain anonymity. Some members have deactivated their personal Twitter accounts due to interactions with the @LamidetFm account to preserve anonymity. They have realised that the commonality of issues can cause them to be easily traced by the police.

While posting messages attacking the government, they connect them to other accounts with the same concerns, especially the accounts of the pressure groups, such as @JogjaBergerak, @BuruhYogyakarta, and @SisterIn-Danger. Connections are also addressed to the accounts of PSIM fans and punk bands, including @CornerAttackYK, @thegenkklitihyk, @BM_BuayaDarat, and @partisjogja.

Conclusion

Musical performances of *Lamidet*'s members have two functions: First, they aim to express their love for underground music and protest against the policies of the Yogyakarta government; second, the stage is a space to bring together people from various places with the same concerns. Through the stage, they influence their fans to support their political actions to criticise the local state, both through street protests and social media. They use social media as an alternative strategy of struggle when street demonstrations threaten them physically. Their political action is the representation of their advocacy of the poor and marginalised urban people of Yogyakarta.

We conclude that, through underground music, *Lamidet* Society has become a galvanizing platform for citizens especially in Yogyakarta. Previously, it was rare that people or certain groups openly criticised the government of Yogyakarta. *Lamidet*'s open resistance is indeed not the first. However, in the era of social media, *Lamidet*'s political actions are important to mention as a new phenomenon.

It has been taboo to criticise or even protest the policy of Kraton (the palace) as the sacred institution, symbol of power, and monarch of Yogyakarta. However, such otherwise forbidden criticisms have found their way into *Lamidet* Society's songs (through the lyrics and music), stage performances, and social media.

References

Baulch, E. (2003). Elsewhere: The Identity Politics of the Balinese Death/Thrash Metal Scene. *Popular Music 22*(2), 195–215.

From Terrace to the Stage. (2019, December 31). From Terrace To The Stage: Live#1 Sidekick [Video]. YouTube. https://www.youtube.com/watch?v=EOJI1XN1NKw

From Terrace to the Stage. (2020, December 31). From Terrace To The Stage: Live#1 Sidekick [Video]. YouTube. https://www.youtube.com/watch?v=EOJI1XN1NKw

Fuchs, C. (2016). Baidu, Weibo and Renren: The Global Political Economy of Social Media in China. *Asian Journal of Communication 26*(1), 14–41.

Fuller, A. (2014). The Struggle for Soccer in Indonesia: Fandom, Archives and Urban Identity. Yogyakarta: Tan Kinira Press.

Jenkins, H. (2006). Confronting the Challenges of Participatory Culture: Media Education for the 21st Century. Cambridge, MA: The MacArthur Foundation.

JITV Pemda DIY. (2018, June 5). Sarasehan | Pengaruh Musik Dalam Bola [Video]. YouTube. https://www.youtube.com/watch?v=QTHqVsHU-_E

Laksono, F., Kasim, H., Kurniawan, N., Mardiya, N. Q., Ramdan, A., & Rachmatika, S. P. (2011). Status Keistimewaan DIY Dalam Bingkai Demokrasi Berdasarkan UUD 45, Jurnal Konstitusi, 8(6), 1059–1086.

Lim, M. (2003). The Internet, Social Networks, and Reform in Indonesia. In N. Couldry and J. Curran (Eds.), Contesting Media Power: Alternative Media in a Networked World (273–288). Lanham, MD: Rowman & Littlefield.

Lukisworo, A., and Sutopo, O. (2017). Metal DIY: Dominasi, Strategi Dan Resistensi. *Jurnal Studi Pemuda 6*(2), 578–589.

Martin-Iverson, S. (2014). Anak Punk Dan Kaum Pekerja: Indonesia punk and class recomposition in urban Indonesia. Draft paper from 'Encountering Urban Diversity in Asia: Class and Other Intersections' workshop (Asia Research Institute, National University of Singapore).

Mitra, A., & Watts, E. (2002). Theorizing Cyberspace: The Idea of Voice Applied to the Internet Discourse. *New Media & Society 4*(4), 479–498.

Moore, R. E. (2013). My Music, My Freedom(?): The Troubled Pursuit of Musical and Intellectual Independence on the Internet in Indonesia. *Asian Journal of Communication 23*(4), 368–385.

Pickles, J. (2000). Punks for peace: Underground music gives young people back their voice. Inside Indonesia. https://www.insideindonesia.org/punks-for-peace

Richter, M. (2012). Musical Worlds in Yogyakarta. Leiden, Netherlands: KITLV Press.

Rifayani, S. D., Harsasto, P., & Martini, R. (2013). Implikasi Kedudukan Gubernur Daerah Istimewa Yogyakarta Terhadap Demokratisasi Dan Efektivitas Pemerintahan Daerah Istimewa Yogyakarta. *Journal of Politic and Government Studies 2*(3), 46–57.

Sen, A. (2010). Music in the Digital Age: Musicians and Fans around the World "Come-Together" on the Net. *Global media Journal 9*. https://www.globalmediajournal. com/open-access/music-in-the-digital-age-musicians-and-fans-around-the-world-come-together-on-the-net.php?aid=35258

Septian, W.T., & Hendrastomo, G. (2020). Musik Indie Sebagai Identitas Anak Muda Di Yogyakarta. *E-Societas 9*(1). https://journal.student.uny.ac.id/societas/article/ view/15778

Sesanti, A. D. (2016). Jogja-Ku (Dune Ora) Didol. Yogyakarta: STPN Press.

Shank, B. (1994). Dissonant Identities: The Rock 'n' Roll Scene in Austin. Texas: Wesleyan University Press.

Stieger, S. (2019). Facebook Usage and Life Satisfaction. *Frontiers Psychology. 10*(2711). https://doi.org/10.3389/fpsyg.2019.02711

Wallach, J. (2003). "Goodbye My Blind Majesty": Music, Language and Politics in the Indonesia Underground. In H. M. Berger and M. T. Carroll (Eds.), Global Pop, Local Language (53–86). Mississippi: University Press of Mississippi.

Wallach, J. (2005). Underground Rock Music: And Democratization in Indonesia. *World Literature Today 79*, 16.

Wallach, J. (2008). Modern Noise, Fluid Genres: Popular Music in Indonesia 1997-2001. Madison: Wisconsin Press.

3 Pseudonymous Influencers and Horny "Alts" in the Philippines

Media Manipulation Be
Media Manipulation beyond
"Fake News"

Jonathan Corpus Ong and Samuel I. Cabbuag

Introduction

Popular journalism about the Philippines' disinformation crisis has often narrowly attributed "fake news" to President Rodrigo Duterte, the Marcos family, and a small but influential army of social media bloggers (Syjuco, 2017). Many online celebrities have indeed amassed thousands of followers by amplifying Duterte's angry populist rhetoric (Curato, 2016) and rallying supporters to embrace a political identity of being part of Duterte's army, known as the "Duterte Death Squad" (DDS) (Gutierrez, 2017). Some of these journalistic reports and academic research have overstated the impact of these supporters on the political process, at times even expressing deterministic claims they were secret weapons for Duterte's electoral victory in 2016 (e.g., Etter, 2017). Senate investigations in past years have pinned the problem of "fake news" on online influencers (Cigaral, 2017), and social media platforms eventually tried to minimise their reach in their News Feed (Rappler. com, 2020). While investigating mega-influencers' popularity illustrates how rabble-rousing and clout-chasing political punditry can be monetised, in reality the disinformation ecosystem goes deeper than those mainstream media have branded as "purveyors of fake news." In the Philippines' competitive disinformation economies, other kinds of micro-influencers have also stepped in to compete for clout and profitable collaborations (see Ong & Cabanes, 2019).

This chapter focuses on the rise of "pseudonymous influencers" and situates them as important, but underreported, disinformation agents that pollute the media ecosystem. Pseudonymous influencers are those innocent-looking parody accounts, humorous meme pages, and romantic love quotes (aka. hugot) accounts that occasionally slip in paid content for their political clients.

While they might not have the same capacities to shape political conversation as a "fake news queen" or traditional celebrity (Robles, 2019), pseudonymous influencers play a unique role in the disinformation economy as their media manipulation strategies are not confined to the narrow frame of "disinformation" or

DOI: 10.4324/9781003619369-4

obvious falsehoods that could be corrected by fact-checkers. Pseudonymous influencers' media manipulations instead take advantage of regulatory loopholes in election campaigns and campaign finance laws. They use humorous language or horny thirsttrap selfies to cloak political messages and even inflammatory speech. They are also able to maintain anonymity that helps them evade both creative industry regulations and official investigations.

Engaging broader debates about the political economy of disinformation (Briant, 2021; Feldstein, 2021) and contributing a Global South case study, our analysis demonstrates that fact-checking initiatives with narrow remits in defining and correcting disinformation must evolve to better respond to local features of disinformation production. What is needed in Southeast Asian countries such as the Philippines are creative and collaborative interventions that can engage private industries as well as promote transparency and accountability in practices of influencer marketing and political campaigning. Researchers and legal experts should collaborate and strategise for local regulatory reform in the promotional industries rather than simply lobby Facebook or Twitter for more or better content moderation of "fake news."

Finally, our chapter contributes to disinformation studies by nuancing how pseudonymous influencers in a personality-based political system test the boundaries of the frame "disinformation." This has far-reaching consequences as these controversial, if not necessarily obviously disinformative, tactics were also used in the failed democratic presidential campaign of Michael Bloomberg in the US (Tiffany, 2020). His campaign assembled armies of social media influencers and meme accounts and raised questions about the professional ethics of campaigning as well as the regulatory grey areas in campaign finance. Several meme pages that Bloomberg enlisted used fake quotes from Bernie Sanders, but the humorous delivery of meme accounts were not as egregiously manipulative as other scandalous tactics in the US election cycle, such as the use of conspiracy theory (Smith & Rosenblatt, 2020). We argue that the media manipulation strategies of pseudonymous influencers have really flown under the radar of disinformation interventions and indeed we need a "whole of society approach" to tackle the issue (Friedberg & Donovan, 2019). The anonymous nature of these accounts is also worth critical reflection: New top-down legislation in the Philippines and other countries in the Global South have pivoted towards banning, censoring, and penalising anonymous accounts on social media with no consideration of the actual content of their pages. Human rights groups such as Article 19 have cautioned that overly punitive legislation threatens users' privacy, freedom of expression, and non-discrimination (Article 19, 2022).

Context and Methods

This chapter draws primarily from a collaborative project we conducted during the 2019 Philippines elections, where we monitored social media conversations and tracked disinformation narratives using digital ethnography between December 2018 and May 2019. Our project was specifically focused on the disinformation agents and media manipulation techniques underreported in mainstream media and escaping the fact-checking interventions that dominate the Philippines' disinformation mitigation space. Together with a larger team of researchers, we observed a range of news pages on various platforms and influencer accounts on Instagram and Twitter. This chapter specifically compiles our insights about the pseudonymous influencers we observed, though we also catalogued a more diverse range of mega- and micro-influencers (see Ong et al., 2019). The broader project made use of mixed methods of qualitative online observations, big data analysis, and interviews with digital campaign strategists to capture evolving trends in election campaigning that include official "above-ground" political advertising and marketing as well as black ops campaigning incorporating disinformation and smear campaigns.

At the same time, this chapter covers the long-term ethnographic research on disinformation economies in the Philippines that involved interviews with a wide range of campaign strategists, influencers, and fake account operators active in digital political campaigns in the 2016 Philippines elections (Ong & Cabanes, 2018, 2019). This original research project used a production studies approach examining the work arrangements and moral justifications of workers behind digital campaigns. This earlier project uncovered the very early use of pseudonymous influencers behind the worldwide trending hashtag #NasaanAngPangulo ("Where Is the President?") smearing the reputation of then-President Benigno Aquino III and spotlighting his absence during a monumental crisis event, as we will discuss further below. As a chapter that provides insights from two election cycles and crisis events happening between campaign periods, we are able to present a typology of the diverse genres of pseudonymous influencers involved in the political process that should inform researchers and policymakers trying to mitigate social media manipulation at scale.

The Pseudonymous Influencer Ecosystem

Influencer is a marketing term used to refer to individuals with a large number of online followers acting as "micro-celebrities" in digital environments (Abidin, 2016). We characterise pseudonymous influencers as part of the influencer economy in the sense that they capitalise on their smaller yet equally fervent organic followers (from 50,000 to 2,000,000 followers). Like other digital influencers, pseudonymous influencers get paid for promoting different commercial brands (Ong & Cabanes, 2018). However, unlike the microcelebrity influencers who are known to capitalise on their "textual and visual narration of their personal lives and lifestyles" (Abidin, 2016, p. 3), pseudonymous influencers operate successfully without disclosing names and identities of their actual operators. As we discuss below, while that pseudonymous[1] influence operations leverage their anonymity to appropriate marginalised identities and use inflammatory speech (Friedberg & Donovan, 2019), it is also the anonymity of pseudonymous influencer accounts that helps them evade industry regulations and serve different political patrons.

This section maps out a diverse ecology of pseudonymous influencers classified to different genres of social media performance and media manipulation strategies: (a) Pinoy Pop Culture Accounts, (b) Parody Accounts, and (c) Horny "Alt" Accounts. The typology presented is based on the characteristics of these accounts and the usual contents they post to appeal and sustain their online audience. By citing examples of disinformation, hate speech, and conspiracy theory seeded by these pseudonymous influencers, we demonstrate how their strategic use of local popular vernaculars and "gutter languages" is able to manoeuvre diverse grey areas around acceptable speech on platforms.

Pinoy Pop Culture Accounts

Pinoy pop culture accounts adopt pseudo personas such as a stereotypical middle-class auntie (e.g., @TitasofManila, or Aunties of Manila), a wise adviser on love and failed romances (e.g., @BobOngQuotes, @hugotquotes), and fictional television villains known for their bitchy (and occasionally misogynist and classist) one-liners (e.g., @SenyoraSantibanez). These accounts comment on Filipino society and culture at large and can reach mega-influencer status of having millions of followers because of their broad *masa* (mass or mainstream) appeal. For instance, Senyora makes fun of herself as a "flat-chested" woman and many of her posts poke fun at well-endowed celebrities and influencers, pushing the boundary of acceptable humour with Filipino gender stereotypes.

Operating mostly on Facebook and Twitter, their media manipulation includes slipping paid posts for their corporate and political clients in between their stream of inspirational or humorous posts. Organised systematically, a team of them can work together and coordinate the tweeting of hashtags according to set schedules in an effort to game the Twitter trending rankings, or more specifically, to secure the top rank in trending topics in order to catch the public's attention.

We first observed this coordinated behaviour on Twitter for #NasaanAng-Pangulo (trans. #WhereIsThePresident) during the Mamasapano Crisis way back in January 2015, which sought to shame President Benigno (Noynoy) Aquino for his absence in the public spotlight in the immediate aftermath of the death of 44 Special Action Force personnel from a failed military operation (see Figure 3.1).

The account @TheBobOngQuote is operated anonymously. The pseudo's persona is that of a wiser old man dispensing generic inspirational quotes. The hashtag #NasaanAngPangulo trended both locally and internationally; both local and international news media outlets such as the BBC picked up the

Figure 3.1 @TheBobOngQuote originated the hashtag #NasaanAngPangulo which trended worldwide on Twitter, and picked up by local and global media outlets.

story and reported heavily on Filipino Twitter publics' anger at an "absentee President" (BBC Trending, 2015). In our analysis of social media discourse, we observed that the @TheBobOngQuote account worked alongside other Pinoy pop culture accounts in a coordinated fashion, and helped shape broader public discussions about the country's need for a populist strongman leader instead of an elite politician. After all, Aquino represented the elite establishment, and his eventual successor Rodrigo Duterte is the angry populist strongman who promised to deliver results during a crisis (Arguelles, 2019). In our ethnographic interviews with campaign strategists (Ong & Cabanes, 2018), one PR consultant took credit for being the brains behind the #NasaanAng-Pangulo influence ops and revealed she "activated" her usual collaborators – a group of younger people operating multiple pseudo accounts – during the crisis. Gaming Twitter trending rankings is a service she has historically offered to corporate clients, which was now being rolled out to political clients.

During our 2019 elections monitoring, we observed similar techniques of assembling pseudonymous influencers, this time to promote campaign slogans for politicians. The most successful hashtag boosting was for Imee Marcos' election campaign slogan #IMEEsolusyon, which reached the top ten trending hashtags on Twitter.

In many ways, pseudonymous influencers' media manipulation strategies enact Alice Marwick and Rebecca Lewis' (2017) concept of attention hacking, which they described as a media manipulation technique employed by US far-right groups that sneak extreme ideas into mainstream media coverage. Attention hackers exploit journalists' predilection to cover newsworthy controversy such as viral and trending topics on Twitter. Our case study here illustrates how innocent-looking pseudonymous influencers similarly hack media and public attention through seeding hashtags for their political clients. In this case, the local attention hackers' practice of gaming Twitter trending topics is primarily driven by corporate marketing logics rather than driven by political beliefs or position (for more on the advertising and PR disinformation work model, see Ong & Cabanes, 2019). As Lee Edwards (2021) argued, PR firms use disinformation "by constructing their meaning in ways that protect professional interests" (p. 177), but at the same time damage the quality of political debate. This is why pseudo accounts can also be inconsistent with their political positions and loyalties – their allegiances can shift and their services can be sold to their client of the moment.

Take, for example, the case of Pinoy pop culture influencers formally enlisted as "endorsers" of politicians (Figure 3.2). Senyora Santibañez, a mega-influencer with over 4.5 million Facebook followers, endorsed reelectionist

Titas of Manila @TitasofManila · Apr 1, 2020   ···
Why are you threatening people's lives at a time like this!!

I have never been angrier at this clown masquerading as this country's leader.

#OustDuterte2020
#OUSTDUTERTENOW

  ○ 14   ⟲ 987   ♡ 2.3K   ↥

Titas of Manila @TitasofManila · Apr 1, 2020   ···
It is tempting to say bad words directed at him out of anger and disgust but I implore you to not stoop down to his level by emanating the same foul mouth he has.

Matutulog na ko pray all good night keep safe love you all

#OustDuterte2020

  ○   ⟲ 65   ♡ 202   ↥

Figure 3.2 In this post, Senyora pokes fun at her physical absence at the book launch of her co-authored joke book with Nancy Binay. Ironically, this account had once bullied Binay and this staged collaboration officially ended their feud and helped reverse the tide of incessant racist/classist bullying of Senator Binay.

Senator Nancy Binay months before the start of the 2019 election campaign season. Prior to this engagement, this account, best known for her snarky take-downs and classist comments on the poor and the working-class, had actually bullied Binay and her family for having dark skin – a racist and classist jibe in postcolonial Philippines where fair skin color is a marker of high status. This is an example of how a politician pays out a powerful influencer to silence their racist and classist bullying, and instead direct their operations to support their political campaigns. In this regard, pseudonymous influencers can be very opportunistic in their political transactions.

Parody Accounts

Unlike Pinoy pop culture accounts whose political loyalties can be more dis-creet unless activated in an official endorsement, parody accounts tend to be obviously supportive or antagonistic towards the politicians or government offices they impersonate.

Parody accounts (such as @NoynoyingAquino, @Korinavirus, and @AltPhilMedia) employ vulgar language when criticising elite establishment personalities and "elite" mainstream media. They attack politicians for being too elitist or lacking political will during times of crisis. Sometimes, they poke fun at specific facial features or personality traits of politicians, such as when @NoynoyingAquino used vulgar humour to call former President Benigno Aquino III mentally abnormal – riffing off an old and very offensive joke that the President looks like a mentally handicapped person.

In the example shown in Figure 3.3, @NoynoyingAquino attacked Aquino and fellow Liberal Party ally current Vice President Leni Robredo, bullied their supporters as being "abnormal" (or mentally handicapped), and praised the Duterte administration.

Meanwhile, anti-Duterte parody accounts – such as Malacañang Events and Catering Services, and the Superficial Gazette of the Republic of the Philippines (parodying official government offices) – use the language of satire and humour to challenge Duterte and his allied authority figures. Rhetorically, parody can be strategically used to poke fun at the excesses and shamelessness of those in power. Sometimes, a target of their parody is how Duterte claims at being a "strongman" politician while actually being cozy with the Chinese government (Shiga & Kawase, 2021).

At times, these parody accounts critical of the Duterte government slipped into racist expressions against Chinese people. For instance, the Malacañang Catering Events and Services account poked fun of Duterte and his close relationship with Xi Jinping, acknowledging how the country is an inch closer to being "a province of China." Other accounts used explicitly racist and crass language. The political parody account Pulitikanginamo (Figure 3.4) regularly referred to Chinese people with the racial slur "ching chong." On one occa-sion, the account misleadingly shared a photo of a Chinese toddler defecating in

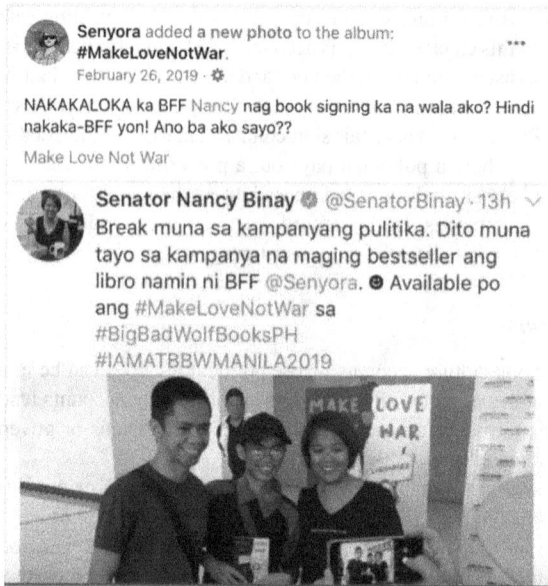

Figure 3.3 A political parody account of former President Benigno Aquino III praised the Duterte administration and attacked his supporters.

public though the incident did not actually occur in a Philippines mall. The page called Chinese tourists "dog eaters" and invited its followers to submit memes mocking them. This page has since been taken down by Facebook after our research team published our study that discussed the use of racist narratives as a political weapon in the 2019 election (see also Silverman et al., 2020).

Figure 3.4 Trans. "Son of a Bitch, these Ching Chongs are so disgusting [profanity]! The beach was closed for months to be cleaned and you'll just make it dirty! You should be banned, you sons of bitches! You're not the only tourists in the world! You sons of bitches you dog eaters! Fuck you! Get out, Ching Chong!" Screenshot by the authors.

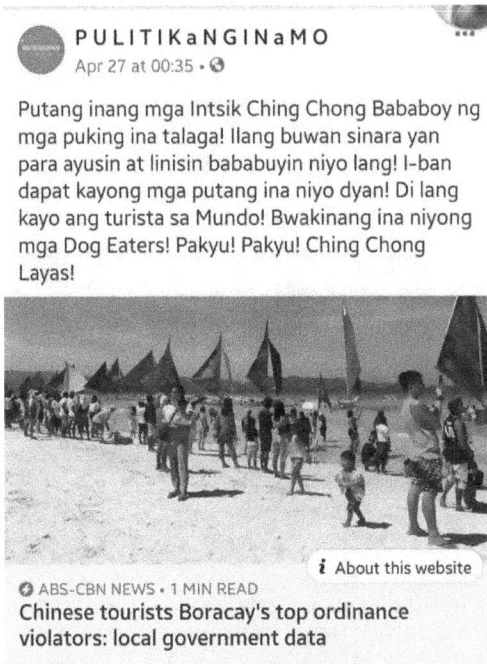

PULITIKaNGINaMO
Apr 27 at 00:35 • ⊙

Putang inang mga Intsik Ching Chong Bababoy ng
mga puking ina talaga! Ilang buwan sinara yan
para ayusin at linisin bababuyin niyo lang! I-ban
dapat kayong mga putang ina niyo dyan! Di lang
kayo ang turista sa Mundo! Bwakinang ina niyong
mga Dog Eaters! Pakyu! Pakyu! Ching Chong
Layas!

i About this website

● ABS-CBN NEWS • 1 MIN READ
**Chinese tourists Boracay's top ordinance
violators: local government data**

Figure 3.5 A discussion between two pseudo accounts discussing the conspiracy theory that
the COVID-19 virus was intentionally leaked from the Wuhan Lab in China.

Like the meme pages in Abidin's study (2018), pseudonymous influencers
can pivot their content during crisis events such as the COVID-19 pandemic
and remain relevant and influential. As shown in the example (Figure 3.5),
pseudonymous influencers were similarly responsible for mixing up conspiracy theory, medical misinformation, and anti-Chinese hate speech in the
Philippines when fears of the virus and its origins took hold. The country has
long been victim to Beijing's territorial encroachments into contested regions
of the West Philippine Sea (Ong, 2021; Tantuco, 2021).

These conspiracy theories are clear examples of what Abidin (2018) describes
as "decision-seeding discourses" that can be expressed in extreme ways by pseudonymous posters and meme pages, while politicians advanced this same narrative in their own official statements in more "moderate" and less inflammatory
tones (for more on anti-Chinese racism in Southeast Asia, see Ong, 2021).

What is critical to highlight here is how pseudonymous influencers' media
manipulation strategies of using anti-China narratives for political gain could
lead to everyday racism and hate, as Chinese migrant workers have been tagged
on social media like in Figures 3.5 and 3.6 as carriers of the virus and agents of
the Chinese government. While these accounts position these racist expressions

Figure 3.6 Alt Account 1 (pseudonym) is an "alt" who shares sexually suggestive content and occasionally participates in political commentary. Here he mixes anti-government commentary #OustDuterteNow and support for LGBTQ equality with #TiteNaSumabog (#EjaculatingPenis) to appeal to a very specific demographic of "woke" horny gay men.

as pockets of resistance, whereby they assert that the Philippines is the primary victim of Chinese territorial aggressions and that it is important that more Filipinos expose and resist political and everyday indignities, these expressions could pose significant threats to multicultural social relations in the country.

Horny "Alt" Porn Accounts

Unlike other platforms with stricter rules around nudity and X-rated content, Twitter has become an "amateur porn paradise" for gay men to experiment with "alter" (i.e., alter ego) personas who are sexually liberated and expressive of their innermost desires. "Alter" accounts in Philippines' Gay Twitter might still act more discreetly than Gay Twitter in the US (Abad-Santos, 2021) as many horny Filipino gay men still hide their faces and adopt pseudonyms to post sexual content, flirt with other "alters," and deep dive into specific sexual genres such as intergenerational or interracial sex. Some "alters" offer paid subscription services on amateur porn sites such as OnlyFans and JustForFans (Cao, 2021). With the popularity of "alters" or "alts" on the rise, some have taken advantage of their huge and passionate fan following for political persuasion.

In the pandemic moment where many have been sexually frustrated while locked down at home, as well as frustrated with the Duterte government's militarised pandemic response, we observed some "alt" porn accounts breaking from their homemade sex video production for political commentary (see Figure 3.6).

In Figure 3.7, we see a similar practice of mixing horny hashtags (#jakol or #masturbate) with a clear anti-Duterte political position. Not only does this help boost the visibility of anti-government voices in the context of a repressive regime, it also connects the alter with other gay men belonging to a minority political camp. As pro-government online trolls and state officials have silenced dissent through digital harassment as well as "redtagging" (insinuating that government critics are Communist sympathisers), maintaining pseudo identities such as alters should be seen as a strategic expression of activism to evade state-sponsored trolling and harassment. We observe alters such as one trans female account (see Figure 3.8) using Twitter to highlight government abuses as well as criticising politically apathetic fellow citizens.

Alter accounts are liberated in both sexual and emotional expressions. We have not gathered material evidence from research interviews that any of the "alt" accounts are formally enlisted as part of paid influence operations, though it is possible that their operators might maintain other meme pages. However, in 2019, we had observed how non-X-rated sexy shirtless men's Instagram pages were activated to repost the official campaign materials for an old male Senator, ostensibly used to micro-target Filipino LGBTQ+ voters

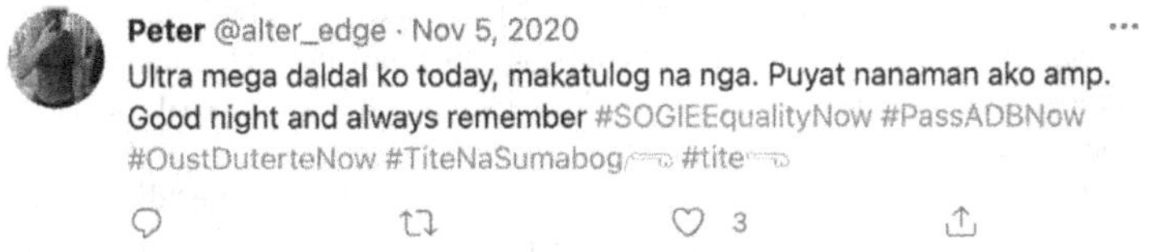
Peter @alter_edge · Nov 5, 2020
Ultra mega daldal ko today, makatulog na nga. Puyat nanaman ako amp.
Good night and always remember #SOGIEEqualityNow #PassADBNow
#OustDuterteNow #TiteNaSumabog #tite
3

Figure 3.7 Alt Account 2 shares their thirst trap photo with hashtags #jakol (#masturbate), #alterph, #OustDuterte, and #OUSTDUTERTENOW as a form of political signaling within their specific community.

Patrick @BossPatrickLang · Sep 22, 2020   ···
GOOD MORNING MGA IDOL 🔥
#jakol #jakolngbinata #alterph #alter #AcademicFreezeNOW
#MentalHealthMatters #OustDuterte #OUSTDUTERNOW #OustDu🔥

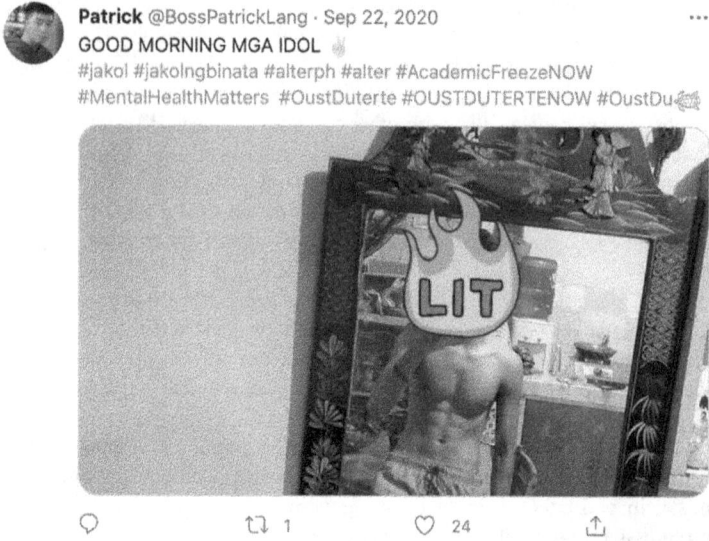

Q   ⟲ 1   ♡ 24   ⬆

Figure 3.8 Alt Account 3 is a trans alter account that mixes pornographic content with
political criticism.

(Ong et al., 2019). This is the most concrete evidence to date that at least one
politician and their political PR team has considered that sexy gay male influencers can arouse a niche voter demographic.

Understanding Local Features of Disinformation to Inform Global Disinformation Interventions

Thus far, this chapter takes a broader view of disinformation shadow economies in the Philippines and spotlights the media manipulation strategies of
pseudonymous influencers that appear entertaining and innocent, while
evading responsibility for stoking racism and seeding crisis narratives.
Pseudonymous influencers are not the disinformation agents most egregiously
responsible for blatantly false news or the most aggressive and inflammatory
speech. However, we have shown examples how they have occasionally used
humour, parody, and horniness to cloak blatantly racist, classist, sexist, or
ableist speech.

At the same time, this chapter exposes the limits of the frame "disinformation" when we discuss the influence operations at play and their many prox-
imities to inauthentic coordinative behaviour, racial targeting and harassment,
"black" campaigning, and attention hacking. As we have shown, pseudonymous influencers can pivot during crisis events such as COVID-19 and seed

"decision-making frames." What this means is that pseudonymous influencers' media manipulation has agility and manoeuvrability to survive and thrive in a sophisticated disinformation economy where platforms, journalists, and fact-checkers focus their energies on catching a select few "purveyors of fake news" but overlooking those enacting subtler and savvier influence operations. This is particularly problematic as platforms' content moderation has been notoriously slow to understand cultural nuances of local humour or niche subcultures. In our experiences when engaging with platforms, their takedown policies are best suited to deplatforming accounts that use specific words, such as racial slurs like "ching chong," as discussed earlier.

Moving forward, we are particularly worried about how these accounts will continue to exploit regulatory loopholes. We observe a lot of momentum behind spotlighting platform accountability in the West, where specific discussions about Silicon Valley platforms' responsibility to deplatform political elites have advanced significantly from previous policies (Zuckerman, 2021). However, the accountability of private industry with the diversity of disinformation-for-hire or influence-for-hire actors lacks steam. It is important that future interventions expand from fact-checking and reporting on false news on social media to include PR firms, advertising agencies, and influencer agencies' responsibility and accountability in the disinformation debate (Briant, 2021; Edwards, 2021). At the same time, civil society groups should resist top-down legislation that caricatures all pseudonymous accounts or anonymous accounts as the source of "fake news," in which some worrying legislation aims to empower law enforcement against anonymous accounts (Article 19, 2022). What is needed are transparency and accountability frameworks rather than overbroad top-down legislation that expands government control and surveillance. In any case, this chapter has presented granular evidence to show how the thriving influencer industries in a Global South context are very much complicit and creative in being enlisted as pawns and artillery for political elites' game of thrones. At the same, because of the anonymous nature of these same accounts, they can be easily scapegoated and targeted by dangerous legislation.

Note

1 Friedberg and Donovan (2019) used the term "psuedoanonymous." Throughout this paper, we used the term "pseudonymous" instead.

References

Abad-Santos, A. (2021, April 16). Gay men helped turn Twitter into an amateur porn paradise. *Vox.* https://www.vox.com/22382428/gay-twitter-alts-nudes-porn.

Abidin, C. (2016). "Aren't These Just Young, Rich Women Doing Vain Things Online?": Influencer Selfies as Subversive Frivolity. *Social Media + Society 2*(2). https://doi.org/10.1177/2056305116641342

Abidin, C. (2018). Internet Celebrity: Understanding Fame Online. Bingley: Emerald Group Publishing.

Arguelles, C. V. (2019). "We Are Rodrigo Duterte": Dimensions of the Philippine Populist Publics' Vote. *Asian Politics & Policy 11*(3), 417–437.

Article 19. (2022, March 9). "Philippines: SIM Card Registration Act undermines online freedoms". Article 19. https://www.article19.org/resources/philippines-sim-card-registration-act-undermines-online-freedoms/

BBC Trending (2015, January 30). "Where is the President?" – a view from the Philippines YouTube. [Video file]. https://www.youtube.com/watch?v=n5z61Rh4G2g

Briant, E. (2021). Lessons from the Cambridge Analytica Crisis: Confronting Today's (Dis)Information Challenges. *The Journal of Intelligence, Conflict, and Warfare 3*(3), 125–127. https://doi.org/10.21810/jicw.v3i3.2775

Cao, R. J. D. (2021). Amateur Porn in Filipino Twitter Alter Community: Affordances, Commodification, Ghettoization, and Gay Masculinity. *Media International Australia 179*(1), 52–65. https://doi.org/10.1177/1329878X211002845

Cigaral, I.N. (2017, October 5). Hits, misses of first Senate probe into fake news. Philstar Global. https://www.philstar.com/headlines/2017/10/05/1745802/hits-misses-first-senate-probe-fake-news

Curato, N. (2016). Politics of Anxiety, Politics of Hope: Penal Populism and Duterte's Rise to Power. *Journal of Current Southeast Asian Affairs 35*(3): 91–109.

Edwards, L. (2021). Organised Lying and Professional Legitimacy: Public Relations' Accountability in the Disinformation Debate. *European Journal of Communication 36*(2), 168–182. https://doi.org/10.1177/0267323120966851

Etter, L. (2017, December 7). What happens when the government uses Facebook as a weapon?. Bloomberg Businessweek. https://www.bloomberg.com/news/features/2017-12-07/how-rodrigo-duterte-turned-facebook-into-a-weapon-with-a-little-help-from-facebook

Feldstein, S. (2021). The Rise of Digital Repression: How Technology Is Reshaping Power, Politics, and Resistance. Oxford: Oxford University Press.

Friedberg, B., & Donovan, J. (2019). On the Internet, Nobody Knows You're a Bot: Pseudoanonymous Influence Operations and Networked Social Movements. *Journal of Design and Science* (6). https://jods.mitpress.mit.edu/pub/2gnso48a/release/8

Gutierrez, N. (2017, August 18). State-sponsored hate: The rise of the pro-Duterte bloggers. Rappler. https://r3.rappler.com/newsbreak/in-depth/178709-duterte-die-hard-supporters-bloggers-propaganda-pcoo

Marwick, A., & Lewis, R. (2017). Media Manipulation and Disinformation Online. New York: Data & Society Research Institute. https://datasociety.net/library/media-manipulation-and-disinfo-online/

Ong, J. C. (2021). The Contagion of Stigmatization: Racism and Discrimination in the "Infodemic" Moment. Social Science Research Council Media Well. https://doi.org/10.35650/MD.2076.d.2021

Ong, J. C., & Cabanes, J. V. C. (2018). Architects of networked disinformation: Behind the scenes of troll accounts and fake news production in the Philippines. Newton Tech4Dev Network. https://newtontechfordev.com/wp-content/uploads/2018/02/ARCHITECTS-OF-NETWORKED-DISINFORMATION-FULL-REPORT.pdf

Ong, J. C., & Cabanes, J. V. (2019). When Disinformation Studies Meets Production Studies: Social Identities and Moral Justifications in the Political Trolling Industry. *International Journal of Communication 13*, 5771–5790. https://ijoc.org/index.php/ijoc/article/view/1141

Ong, J. C., Tapsell, R., & Curato, N. (2019). Tracking digital disinformation in the 2019 Philippine midterm elections. New Mandala. https:/newmandala.org/disinformation

Robles, R. (2019, May 15). Philippine midterm elections: Mocha Uson, 'queen of fake news', fails to win House seat. South China Morning Post. https://www.scmp.com/week-asia/politics/article/3010373/philippine-midterm-elections-mocha-uson-queen-fake-news-fails

Shiga, Y., & Kawase, K. (2021, July 27). Duterte stresses soft approach toward China in last policy speech. Nikkei. https://asia.nikkei.com/Politics/International-relations/South-China-Sea/Duterte-stresses-soft-approach-toward-China-in-last-policy-speech

Silverman, C., Lytyvnenko, J., & Kung, W. (2020, January 7). Disinformation for hire: How a new breed of PR firms is selling lies online. Buzzfeed News. https://www.buzzfeednews.com/article/craigsilverman/disinformation-for-hire-black-pr-firms?utm_source=dynamic&utm_campaign=bfsharecopy

Smith, A., & Rosenblatt, K. (2020, March 4). Bloomberg's novel meme strategy is drawing the wrong kind of buzz. NBC News. https://www.nbcnews.com/tech/social-media/bloomberg-s-novel-meme-strategy-drawing-wrong-kind-buzz-n1146626

Syjuco, M. (2017, October 24). Fake news floods the Philippines. New York Times. https://www.nytimes.com/2017/10/24/opinion/fake-news-philippines.html?smid=url-share

Tantuco, V. (2021, May 22). Philippines, China meet as South China Sea tensions flare. Rappler. https://www.rappler.com/nation/philippines-china-meet-south-china-sea-tensions-flare-may-2021

Tiffany, K. (2020, February 28). You can't buy memes. The Atlantic. https://www.theatlantic.com/technology/archive/2020/02/bloomberg-memes-instagram-ads/607219/

Zuckerman, E. (2021, August 31). Demand five precepts to aid social media watchdogs. Nature. https://www.nature.com/articles/d41586-021-02341-9

4 Studying Private Messaging Groups

Misinformation in WhatsApp Family Group Chats, and Research Regimes in Singapore(ans)

Crystal Abidin and Natalie Pang

WhatsApp Cultures in Singapore

Singapore has one of the highest smartphone ownership rates in the world (Liu et al., 2016, p. 145), with 91% of the adult population owning a smartphone in comparison to 71% who own laptops or desktop computers (Chen & Neo, 2019, p. 3). As such, while WhatsApp has a high penetration use in Southeast Asia at large (Faisal et al., 2019, p. 45), it is no surprise that WhatsApp has been consistently identified in reports as being the most popular messaging app used in Singapore (Chen & Neo, 2019).

While there are varieties of family interest groups on WhatsApp, each offering resources and a forum for members to congregate, some have provided unique insights into family and parenting culture in Singapore. A recent example includes "mummy WhatsApp groups" where mothers share ideas and tips about disciplining their children during the pandemic-induced extended period of self-isolation and home-based learning, featuring discussions about where to purchase or even bulk buy rattan canes (Neogy, 2021). Perhaps a more positive example includes organisations seeking to promote "wholesome family-friendly values" via WhatsApp like the WhatsApp Autism Community Singapore (n.d.) that claims to be the country's "largest public WhatsApp network for the autism community."

Evidently, WhatsApp is a central app for the middle-aged and older cohorts in Singapore, and this has been recognised by the state. Citizens have been invited to make the Gov.sg WhatsApp service their "first stop" for all updates including "Key Government Announcements" such as the Budget, and "Factually" which provides "clarifications on widespread fake news" about government policies (Gov.sg, 2020). The COVID-19 pandemic further instituted the integration of WhatsApp into the daily communication repertoire of Singaporean citizens, as several WhatsApp-based initiatives were launched and promoted by the government. For instance, the Gov.sg WhatsApp account was updated to allow citizens to subscribe for "timely and trusted updates" about the pandemic in the country's four official languages; this was designed

DOI: 10.4324/9781003619369-5

by "GovTech" or Government Technology Agency, a statutory board of the Singapore government nestled under the Prime Minister's Office as part of a "suite of digital tools" to manage the pandemic (GovTech Singapore, 2021).

The Singapore government's swift allocation of resources to facilitate better communication via WhatsApp, especially to reach the older cohorts of "Boomers" (those born between 1946 and 1964) is not unfounded. It has been observed by reporters and commentators that members of this age cohort have been chiefly responsible for fear mongering, sending on unverified forwarded message chains, and perhaps unwittingly spreading misinformation (Yeoh, 2020) despite their well-meaning intentions. In response, some brands have even decided to address this target demographic head-on, by introducing "Boomer-friendly hygiene messages" in the format of Boomer-styled WhatsApp memes – described as "floral or religious in nature," featuring "kitschy fonts" and "random graphics," that are generally "tacky" and "old-fashioned" – in the hopes that their marketing strategy would circulate prominently in family group chats (Sholihyn, 2020).

Considering the centrality of WhatsApp among Singaporean families' communication cultures, and the norms of Boomers and their propensity for forwarding on chain mail and memes without verification, this chapter provides an in-depth look at private messaging groups like WhatsApp and the unwitting or well-intended misinformation that flows through networks of care.

WhatsApp Domestication and Misinformation through Networks of Care

WhatsApp is one of the fastest growing social media platforms globally, and in Singapore, it has emerged as the top social media platform in 2021 (Statista, 2023b). The popularity and adoption of platforms such as WhatsApp may be explained using what Pang and Schauder (2007) have identified as the PC/I, or the Personal Computing/Internet threshold, at the turn of an era of parallel advances in both personal/mobile computing and broadband internet infrastructure. Singapore has been one of the most active countries in identifying and working towards the PC/I threshold, with extensive IT plans, public education initiatives in digital literacy, and personal computing plans such as the Digital Access@Home (Infocomm Media Development Authority, 2023). Collectively, these initiatives and IT plans worked to contribute to a highly connected population, with around 88.5% of the Singapore population reported to be using the internet in 2020 (Statista, 2021). In particular, the growth of WhatsApp has been significant, with an estimate of 4.81 million users in Singapore in 2021 (Statista, 2023a) out of a total population of 5.45 million people in the same year.

The growth of WhatsApp especially in everyday communication may be understood using the concept of domestication (Matassi et al., 2019). As a concept developed to reject technological determinism, Silverstone (2006, p. 233) argued that domestication can be deployed to understand the process of "bringing things home… analyzed in the negotiations of ownership and control of both new and old machines and the consumption of content, within the micro-pores of the domestic setting and in the family or household relationship…."

Consequently, domestication involves individuals bringing communication technologies to their domestic lives and routines, and comprises four stages: Appropriation, conversion, incorporation, and objectification. *Appropriation* refers to the practice of making sense of technologies that users are acquiring in their lives, while conversion points to the ways in which "an artifact is negotiated and inserted into broader relations" (Matassi et al., 2019, p 2191). While appropriation may be used to understand how users normalise WhatsApp in everyday life, *conversion* alludes to one's social membership (or lack of) through the chat groups that one has on the platform. Researching WhatsApp often involves contextualising the platform through two initial lenses. At the level of appropriation, the study of WhatsApp should involve understanding the drivers and motivations for individuals to incorporate the platform in the activities of everyday life. This should also include understanding the affordances of the platform as perceived by individuals. At the level of conversion, the focus is on the composition of chat groups – often reflective of how WhatsApp is used to facilitate as well as to mediate social networks and relationships.

Referring to routines in which technologies are used, *incorporation* may be used to understand temporalities associated with WhatsApp – what time of the day it is used, what routines it is used for. Alongside incorporation, *objectification* seeks to understand the spatiality associated with technologies – with WhatsApp, this concept provides a means to articulate the spatiality of WhatsApp itself, not just where it is used but also how WhatsApp has become a platform of many gatherings. As Matassi et al. (2019, p. 2193) pointed out through their study, WhatsApp "has become a place in itself." Both incorporation and objectification provide additional guiding questions and analytical lenses, as WhatsApp is explored as not just how it is used (temporalities) but also how it functions as a platform for spatial interactions (objectification).

Matassi et al.'s (2019) study revealed the domestication of WhatsApp as a central means for everyday communication in Argentina, and its use being shaped by the life stages that users associate themselves with. This has implications in terms of introducing strong and weak ties into the groups, as well as being perceived as "a highly versatile, all-encompassing space of encounter, meaning-making, and coordination where entrance barriers are low and exit costs are high" (Matassi et al., 2019, p. 2195). Their findings addressed extant scholarly gaps in the literature which are often focused on the digital practices of youths. For instance, Waterloo et al.'s (2018) study on adolescents and young adults' use of WhatsApp found that the platform is often used for strong tie-networks, and positive and negative emotions are often exchanged due to the presence of strong ties.

These studies advance the understanding of the role of WhatsApp in everyday communication for different populations. Matassi et al.'s (2019) work also alludes to the objectification of WhatsApp as a cultural and material object especially within the household, where meanings are being made about relationships, conversations, as well as an object. Similar observations have also been made, for instance, about older users who reflect on how WhatsApp chat groups with their children can strengthen their relationships, with the milestone of boyfriends or girlfriends being added to family chats as "the equivalent of marriage" (Donoughue, 2019).

Such reflections allude to networks of care within which misinformation is embedded – specifically, family networks that use WhatsApp to develop social interactions and to maintain familial ties. "Family" is considered broadly to also include extended families, non-blood, and kindred ties that are associated with one's consciousness and response of care. This drives the dissemination and flow of misinformation through family chats on WhatsApp. In this chapter, we share reflections on how the socio-technical approach informs our research findings, as well as the regimes shape our work.

Methodology

Our research context comprised 30 personal interviews complemented by the "social media scroll back method" (Robards & Lincoln, 2017), which were all conducted in person in 2019. This included two groups: Group One comprised 20 individuals (citizens and residents) in Singapore who were interviewed by the second author and their research assistant, and Group Two comprised 10 Singaporean migrants and diaspora in Australia who were interviewed by the first author. The design of the interview schedule and scroll back guide was led by the first author. Both groups were active users of WhatsApp to keep in touch with various social groups, but especially nuclear and extended family units. For the latter group of migrants, WhatsApp played a critical role in facilitating and maintaining communication – both pragmatic and phatic – for family units who had been living apart for extended periods of time.

Interviewees in Group One were recruited through an advertisement inviting research participants at a university. Interviewees in Group Two were recruited via snowball sampling from a migrant church in Australia with a high population of Singaporean diaspora. The research team aimed for a representative spread of gender, race, and age among the interviewees as much as possible. Due to the recruitment approach at a university in Group One, the sample consisted of younger participants in their 20s, and skewed towards women who had responded to the call for research participants more actively than did men. However, the age range tended to be higher in Group Two as interviewees were migrants and diaspora who were in a later life stage from having

Table 4.1 Summary of interviewee demographics

Grouping	Gender	Race	Age
Group One	Male: 5 Female: 15	Chinese: 14 Malay, Indian, Others: 6	18–19yo: 1 20–29yo: 15 30–39yo: 1 40–49yo: 1 50–59yo: 2
Group Two	Male: 6 Female: 4	Chinese: 8 Malay, Indian, Others: 2	20–29yo: 2 30–39yo: 7 40–49yo: 1

immigrated to establish their own nuclear families in Australia. The demographic background of our interviewees is briefly tabulated below (Table 4.1):

All interviews were conducted in English and took between 20 minutes and 1 hour. Personal interviews were recorded via an audio device and transcribed for coding and analysis. Scroll backs were recorded via the video function on the interviewers' smartphones and visually analysed for text and image (e.g. pictures, gifs, short videos); however, six informants opted not to have their scroll backs recorded on video, and interviewers took field notes as a substitute.

Reflecting on the "Socio-Technical"

In a society that has always recognised technological innovations and advances as key drivers of development and change, we are often confronted by questions associated with the tendency for us to posit or explain the impacts of emerging technologies. In our own project, it is not one way or the other; that is, the affordances of technologies must also be recognised alongside individual and social practices of technologies. This brings us to the focus on studying the socio-technical.

Meyer (2014, p. 57) posited that in considering the "socio-technical" aspects of studying technology, the hyphen is instrumental in guiding researchers towards a "balanced view toward the relative importance of the social and the technical aspects of any given socio-technical construct." Drawing on the meaning of the hyphen, this means that our study of WhatsApp must not only be intentional in moving away from *a priori* assumptions of the platform and its effects, but also carefully consider a balanced view between technological determinism and social considerations including how people shape the technologies they use.

The development of the hyphen manifested in two ways for us in our research. Theoretically, the application of domestication theory provided a rigorous pair of lenses to evaluate the affordances of WhatsApp, agency, as well as the temporal and spatial aspects of WhatsApp use in households through appropriation, conversion, incorporation, and objectification. Methodologically, the use of the scroll back method has been instrumental in allowing for other questions to be asked, and grounding conversations in key, pivotal moments of WhatsApp use in the context of family networks manifested as chat groups. This also provided a means for researchers to "safely" challenge and question the participant's recall, truth-making, and sense-making. Doing this is essential especially in terms of the researcher shifting from a role of information solicitor to becoming a critical peer, inviting participants to review and challenge their own digital practices, ethos, and memories. For many participants, this approach provided an opportunity to reflect on WhatsApp as a place for communication as well as on its role in navigating misinformation embedded in intra and inter-generational family communication.

Focusing on the hyphen is also helpful in addressing one of the key methodological problems arising with studying non-tangible objects such as WhatsApp. As Livingstone (2007, p. 19) pointed out, these objects can be material as well as non-material, and "the challenge remains to sustain a subtle analysis of both the domestic context of use and the semiotic richness of the online world that people engage in; in the turn away from text towards context… it is the former that gets lost." In the case of studying private messaging platforms like WhatsApp, this means that the broader domestic context of use must not be forgotten in the pursuit of analysing what happens on WhatsApp. The scroll back provides a means for researchers to systematically review what is happening on the screen as well as beyond the screen.

To illustrate this point, the following is a redacted exchange between one of us and a participant in her early-30s in the study, who was recalling a time when a meme was circulated in her extended family chat group:

Interviewer: So you were telling me about the meme? Could you share more about it and why you remember it?

Participant: Well, it was not just because it was funny… but it also contained some fake news, you know, that was circulating at that time.

Interviewer: How did you respond to it?

Participant: I think many of us in the group responded with the laughter emoji. I did too, but I think I also pointed out that it was false.

Interviewer: Could you scroll back to that moment again?

Participant: [after scrolling back] No… wait, I did not really respond. Come to think of it, I was never really comfortable with responding in that chat… so many aunties and uncles there.

The scroll back interview provided an opportunity for the researcher to gather pivotal moments of WhatsApp use by reviewing content that is otherwise ephemeral and undocumented in studies of instant messaging platforms. Additionally, the researcher was also able to invite the participant to not only critically reflect on her own responses earlier, but unveil power dynamics in the social relationships she has with relatives in the chat group.

Regimes Guiding Our Research

As our project wrapped up, it became clear that ethical research in our field sites were guided by specific socio-cultural, political, and ethical regimes. Firstly, as a *multi-sited project* with fieldwork in both Singapore and Australia, we were also confronted with the challenge to bracket interview responses with broader contexts of identity. Identity is, of course, multi-faceted. This is sometimes manifested as class with more affluent and highly educated participants giving quite well-informed perspectives compared to others who may not. Such bracketed connotations of identity accompany our analysis, as it implies that the analysis extends well beyond what is being said. Who-said-what and the underlying social dynamics embedded within each WhatsApp group become central to our analysis of how individuals navigate and respond to misinformation.

Secondly, the wider context of our study was *ethnographic* in nature, paying heed to the demographic and situational context of our informants, including concerns and tensions that played out along gendered, racial, and generational fault lines. The active and ongoing consent that we had obtained from our informants throughout the personal interviews, scroll back sessions, and larger context of (digital) ethnography allowed us to maintain our ethos of purposive sampling. This prioritised voices and perspectives from the "margins," where we could centre in on the folklore of governmentality, and place weight on gossip and hearsay as the media through which citizens air their concerns about state surveillance and intrusion.

Thirdly, the coding of our discursive data was attentive "*decoding*" *double-speak and code switching,* in acknowledgement of the self-censorship practised by Singaporeans when topics skirted between mainstream and fringed perspectives. As researchers, analysing the narratives also involves identifying what are mainstream discourses and what may be fringe narratives or perspectives. Doing so enables us to critically engage our participants, inviting them to explore other positions or perspectives. It is also essential to acknowledge that digital information literacy in Singapore is often dominated by state-run campaigns and literacy programmes that are developed and run regularly. This means that most of our participants – even the ones that are not residing in Singapore – were able to give "textbook" answers that are well-known. In other words, they are highly astute and aware of what are the best practices are, and what they ought to be doing and saying. Our fieldwork would often entail peeling back this instinctive way of re-sponding, to get participants to share and reflect on the actual realities of dealing with misinformation. The scroll back interview provides a key means to do this.

Finally, to pry open a space that allowed interviewees to feel comfortable with expressing their scepticism, some interview questions and follow-up prompts were deliberately positioned as coming from an ally and antagonist, respectively. The "researcher standpoint" that we had overtly performed was extrapolated and assumed by interviewees as a "guiding track" for specific narratives that they had assumed we were soliciting, rather than genuinely reflecting on the reality of their everyday practices (as evidenced in the scroll back corroboration against the interview data above). As such, the alternating *in- and out-group identifications* between interviewees and researchers provided opportunities for the former to adjust or recalibrate their footing, standpoints, or stances, as the conversation developed beyond "textbook" template answers.

Acknowledgements

The production of this research was supported by a 2019 Facebook Integrity Foundational Research Award for a project titled "Decoding the Weaponizing of Pop Culture on WhatsApp in Singapore and Malaysia."

References

Chen, J., & Neo, P. (2019). Texting the Waters: An Assessment of Focus Groups Conducted via the WhatsApp Smartphone Messaging Application. *Methodological Innovations 12*(3), 1–10. https://doi.org/10.1177/2059799119884276

Donoughue, P. (2019, December 26). *As Facebook pivots to private, the family group chat becomes a weird staple of contemporary life.* ABC NEWS. https://www.abc.net.au/news/2019-12-26/as-facebook-pivots-to-private,-family-group-chats-fire-up/11789028

Faisal, S., Nor, A., & Abdullah, N. H. (2019). Persuasive System Design for Global Acceptance of Smartphone Apps. *Procedia Computer Science 152*, 44–50. https://doi.org/10.1016/j.procs.2019.05.025

Gov.sg. (2020, March 17). *Gov.sg on WhatsApp: How to Sign Up.* https://www.gov.sg/article/govsg-on-whatsapp

GovTech Singapore. (2021, August 17). *Responding to COVID-19 with Tech.* https://www.developer.tech.gov.sg/our-digital-journey/singapore-digital-government-journey/tech-for-public-good/combatting-covid19-with-tech.html

Infocomm Media Development Authority. (2023, April 14). *Digital Access@Home.* https://www.imda.gov.sg/dah

Liu, M.-H., Margaritis, D., & Zhang, Y. (2016). Competition and Petrol Pricing in the Smartphone Era: Evidence from Singapore. *Economic Modelling 53*, 144–155. https://doi.org/10.1016/j.econmod.2015.11.020

Livingstone, S. (2007). On the Material and the Symbolic: Silverstone's Double Articulation of Research Traditions in New Media Studies. *New Media & Society 9*(1), 16–24.

Matassi, M., Boczkowski, P. J., & Mitchelstein, E. (2019). Domesticating WhatsApp: Family, Friends, Work, and Study in Everyday Communication. *New Media & Society 21*(10), 2183–2200. https://doi-org.libproxy1.nus.edu.sg/10.1177/1461444819841890

Meyer, E. T. (2014). Examining the Hyphen: The Value of Social Informatics for Research and Teaching. In P. Fichman & H. Rosenbaum (Eds.), *Social Informatics: Past, Present and Future* (pp. 57–74). Newcastle, UK: Cambridge Scholarly Publishers.

Neogy, S. (2021, May 19). *Singapore mum WhatsApp groups ablaze with chats on cane shops and assessment books for kids.* Yahoo!Style. https://sg.style.yahoo.com/singapore-mum-whatsapp-groups-ablaze-083429132.html

Pang, N., & Schauder, D. (2007). The Culture of Information Systems in Knowledge-Creating Contexts: The Role of User-Centred Design. Informing Science: The International Journal of an Emerging Transcipline 10, 203–235. https://doi.org/10.28945/466.

Robards, B., & Lincoln, S. (2017). Uncovering Longitudinal Life Narratives: Scrolling Back on Facebook. *Qualitative Research 17*(6), 715–730. https://doi.org/10.1177/1468794117700707

Sholihyn, I. (2020, April 20). Have Some Boomer-Friendly Hygiene Tips to Share in Family Group Chats, Courtesy of Lifebuoy. *AsiaOne.* https://www.asiaone.com/digital/have-some-boomer-friendly-hygiene-tips-share-family-group-chats-courtesy-lifebuoy

Silverstone, R. (2006). Domesticating Domestication: Reflections on the Life of a Concept. In T. Berker, M. Hartmann, M. Punie & Y. Ward (Eds.), *Domestication of Media and Technology. Maidenhead* (pp. 229–248). Open University Press, Maidenhead, UK.

Statista. (2021). Share of population using the internet in Singapore from 2010 to 2020 and a forecast up to 2026. https://www-statista-com.libproxy1.nus.edu.sg/statistics/975069/internet-penetration-rate-in-singapore/

Statista. (2023a). Number of WhatsApp users in Singapore from 2019 to 2028. https://www-statista-com.libproxy1.nus.edu.sg/forecasts/1145919/whatsapp-users-in-singapore

Statista. (2023b). Penetration rate of top social networks in Singapore as of the 3rd quarter of 2022. https://www.statista.com/statistics/284466/singapore-social-network-penetration/

Waterloo, S. F., Baumgartner, S. E., & Peter, J. (2018). Norms of Online Expressions of Emotion: Comparing Facebook, Twitter, Instagram, and WhatsApp. *New Media & Society 20*(5), 1813–1831. https://doi.org/10.1177/1461444817707349

WhatsApp Autism Community Singapore. (n.d.). [WACS is Singapore's largest public WhatsApp network for the autism community]. *https://whatsapp.iautistic.com/*

Yeoh, G. (2020, February 1). This FB group satirises how boomers speak about the coronavirus. Hilarious or harmful? *Yahoo!Style.* https://sg.style.yahoo.com/fb-group-satirises-boomers-speak-064732474.html

Conclusion

Internet Research and the Way Forward

Natalie Pang and Crystal Abidin

> I knew who I was this morning, but I've changed a few times since then.
> (Lewis Carroll, in Alice's Adventures
> in Wonderland/Through the Looking Glass)

This edited collection brings together scholars conducting research on (everyday) politics in Southeast Asia via networks of internet popular culture. In this collection, we ask: What adaptations do researchers have to deal with when contextualising their research within and across socio-political-techno-logical contexts, and how they shape researchers and their practices? Moving forward, what are key trends and dynamics in Southeast Asia that can impact such adaptations?

Reflecting on these key questions, we bring to the surface our own challenges and contemplate the way forward in internet research. Southeast Asia is well-known for its cultural diversity, but with it comes difficulties in identifying common nomenclature and topics with which researchers and studies can engage in a way that is recognised as meaningful. From the collection, it was also apparent that researchers had diverse epistemological assumptions about research in Southeast Asia. This is as much a reflection of the different disciplinary backgrounds that researchers come from, as it is also a reflection of the diverse socio-political-technological contexts shaping the use of the internet in Southeast Asia.

Emerging Trends in Internet Research

Perhaps the challenges may explain some gaps that have emerged based on the extant literature, which allude to directions for future internet research in Southeast Asia. For instance, Poulsen et al. (2024), in their scoping review of digital rights and mobile health in Southeast Asia, found little research engaging with topics associated with digital rights. Essentially, the finding shows a lack of engagement and indifference to the concept of digital rights and data privacy on the part of researchers as well as citizens. While the chapter on

DOI: 10.4324/9781003619369-6

Malaysia (Pauline Pooi Yin Leong) explored the topic, more research is evidently needed in these areas, including methodological innovations to unpack the meaning of digital rights.

The practice of digital citizenship is also gaining ground and evolving in Southeast Asia. Here, we adopt Yue et al.'s (2019) development of digital citizenship, in seeing citizenship as "practice through which civic activities in the various dimensions of citizenship are conducted" (p. 100). Through this lens, researchers examine the use of the internet in the contexts of civic participation and practice, juxtaposing them against more conservative and traditional socio-political cultures. This is evident in the chapters on Indonesia (Muria Endah Sokowati and Fajar Junaedi) and the Philippines (Jonathan Corpus Ong and Samuel Cabbuag). Research in this area is forthcoming, with researchers such as Hanckel (2023) exploring how queer youths in Southeast Asia use the internet to "make sense of their experiences and ongoing stigma and discrimination" (p. 1).

Enactments of citizenship and democratisation in Southeast Asia are deeply dialogical – practices of digital citizenship are shaped by socio-political-technological structures, but also actively shape the development of the very same structures in Southeast Asia. This is reflected in the chapter on Singapore (Crystal Abidin and Natalie Pang). In other words, while practices of digital citizenship are often enabled or sanctioned by their respective social, political, and technological contexts, these practices can impact interactions and functioning of society, development and governance of technological platforms, and even the development of political systems. While the internet affords opportunities to grow towards greater inclusivity and deliberation, they may also be used by the state for surveillance and addressing dissent (Alami et al., 2023). Other than being deeply aware of the socio-political nuances driving what they see on the internet, researchers need to be mindful of how to approach the research, including research subjects. Insights on this issue in various contexts are offered in all of the chapters in this book, but more work needs to be done as democracies in Southeast Asia are rapidly evolving.

AI and Research in Southeast Asia

Developments around and the growth of artificial intelligence (AI), especially generative AI, have introduced opportunities as well as significant challenges for research. While generative AI tools offer benefits such as summarising information quickly, making it possible to synthesise large datasets as well as making more information accessible, risks associated with misinformation and malinformation, hallucinations, and ethics are significant.

As Putra (2024) noted, ASEAN nations have not cultivated a "regional governance framework" to address the challenges of AI, despite its potential to "accelerate GDP" among member states. The gaps in developing an AI regulatory framework in Southeast Asia are driven by a number of factors, including but not limited to lack of AI expertise, insufficient awareness and trust in AI, and inadequate infrastructure (Lian, 2023). However, business strategists have suggested that Southeast Asian nations generally value the principles of "diversity, inclusivity, and sustainability" which can encourage the region to develop AI regulations that are "human-centric and value-based" and "risk-based and context-specific" (Lian, 2023). Still, the lack of a governance framework and regulations contributes to concerns over ethical and privacy concerns for internet researchers, including a lack of consensus over how researchers may use AI.

The scholarship has noted the "imbalanced global participation" of nations in the Global Partnership on Artificial Intelligence (GPAI), with Singapore being the only member from Southeast Asia (Keith, 2024). Yet a "comparative policy analysis" has revealed that the AI governance policies of Southeast Asians are "largely compatible" regardless of GPAI membership (Keith, 2024). A study has found that the AI policies of Southeast Asian nations generally focus on two main areas: Ethics (e.g. Singapore) and human capital development (e.g. Indonesia, Malaysia, Thailand, Vietnam) (Keith, 2024). Given the diversity across the Southeast Asian nations, there is some pushback in the region, with Islamic business experts cautioning the need to analyse the "dominance of technological rationality over Islamic morality," to ensure that frameworks cultivating AI advancements in Muslim Southeast Asia are aligned with Islamic moral and ethical standards (Anoraga, 2024).

In academia, Singapore leads the region on AI research in educational settings, and a review of the scholarship on Scopus has recommended that Southeast Asia must focus its future AI research on computer aided instruction, chatbots, ChatGPT, assessments, and generative AI (Zafrullah et al., 2024). In many ways, AI tools make research more accessible in that they lower the barriers of entry for researchers, but at the same time, heavy reliance on using AI to generate responses to complex research questions can lead to uncritical engagement with research and data presented, and weaken researchers' ability to gather primary data. Because AI is driven by internet connectivity and internet use, researchers need to critically reflect on the use of AI in both their research practices and emerging topics (e.g. AI generated deep fakes), as well as equip themselves with relevant competencies.

References

Alami, A. N., Luong, D. N. A., Prihatini, E., Ramadhani, E., Go, J. R. R., Hafidzah, N., & Atiyah, U. 2023. Democratization in the Digital Era: Experience from Southeast Asia. *JAS (Journal of ASEAN Studies) 10*(2). https://doi.org/10.21512/jas.v10i2.9361

Anoraga, B. 2024. The future of Artificial Intelligence in/and of Islam: A View from Muslim Southeast Asia. *Journal of Islamic and Muslim Studies 9*(1): 115–123. https://doi.org/10.2979/jims.00031

Hanckel, B. 2023. Queer Youth and Digital Technologies in Southeast Asia. In B. Hanckel (Ed.), *LGBT+ Youth and Emerging Technologies in Southeast Asia. Perspectives on Children and Young People*, 14. Singapore: Springer. https://doi. org/10.1007/978-981-99-4394-4_1

Keith, Andrew J. 2024. Governance of Artificial Intelligence in Southeast Asia. *Global Policy 15*(5): 937–954. https://doi.org/10.1111/1758-5899.13458

Lian, Anndy. 2023. "Why Southeast Asia needs to collectively harness AI." *International Policy Digest,* 13 December. https://intpolicydigest.org/why-southeast-asia-needs-to-collectively-harness-ai/

Poulsen, A., Song, Y. J., Fosch-Villaronga, E., LaMonica, H. M., Iannelli, O., Alam, M., & Hickie, I. B. 2024. Digital Rights and Mobile Health in Southeast Asia: A Scoping Review. *Digital Health 10.* https://doi.org/10.1177/20552076241257058

Putra, B. A. 2024. Governing AI in Southeast Asia: ASEAN's Way Forward. *Frontiers in Artificial Intelligence 7.* https://doi.org/10.3389/frai.2024.1411838

Yue, A., Nekmat, E., & Beta, A. 2019. Digital Literacy Through Digital Citizenship: Online Civic Participation and Public Opinion Evaluation of Youth Minorities in Southeast Asia. *Media and Communication 7*(2): 100–114. https://doi.org/10.17645/mac.v7i2.1899

Zafrullah, S., Kumala Sembiring, Y., Ramadana, N., Nuralisa Gunawan, R., & Kusuma-wardhani, K. 2024. Research Trends on the Use of Artificial Intelligence in Educational Environments in Southeast Asia on Scopus Database: A Bibliometric Analysis (2014–2024). *Innovative: Journal of Social Science Research 4*(5): 8972–8989.

Index

62   *Index*

gay men *see* LGBTQ+
generative AI 59; *see also* artificial
    intelligence (AI)
global disinformation interventions
    42–43
Global Partnership on Artificial
    Intelligence (GPAI) 59

Hamengku Buwono X, Sultan of
    Yogyakarta 22
Hanckel, B. 58
hate speech: anti-Chinese 39;
    definitions of 12; and
    trolling 2, 6–9, 11–13
Hendrastomo, G. 24

#IMEEsolusyon 35
incorporation, domestication
    stage of 49
Indonesia 2, 19–20, 22, 23;
    see also music; Yogyakarta
influencers *see* pseudonymous
    influencers
information and communication
    technologies (ICTs) 1, 5;
    see also technologies
Instagram 3, 21, 22, 25, 26, 33, 41
internet: and communication
    technology 22; hate speech and
    trolling 6–9, 11–13; popular culture
    1–4; research 5, 57–58; and social
    media 6; users 20–21

Jenkins, H. 20
Jinping, Xi 37
JOOX 22
journalists/journalism 6, 31, 36, 43;
    see also media
Junaedi, Fajar 2
JustForFans 41

Kusuma, Adnan 21–24, 26, 27

Lamidet Society 2, 19–28; autonomy of
    25–26; criticism 22–23; introduction
    19–21; local football supporters 23;
    method 21; musical performance
    (*see* music); political actions
    (*see* politics); social media 26–27;
    stage of protest 23–24; underground
    scene 21–22
Law No. 13/2012 22, 27
Law on the Job Creation Act 26

Leong, P. P. Y. 2
Lewis, Rebecca 36
LGBTQ+ 40–41
Lim, M. 20
Livingstone, S. 52
Lukisworo, A. 24

Malacañang Events and Catering
    Services 37
Malay-Muslim community 7–11
Malaysia 5–14; contentious
    communication in 6–9; hate
    speech and trolling 2, 6–9, 11–13;
    introduction 5–6; methodological
    issues in 9–13; research process
    (*see* research/researcher);
    social media (*see* social media);
    socio-political issues in 6–7
Malaysiakini 2, 8, 9, 12
Marcos, Imee 35
Martin-Iverson, S. 24
Marwick, Alice 36
Matassi, M. 49, 50
media 31–43; digital 5, 7; manipulation
    (*see* pseudonymous influencers);
    social 5–14; *see also* journalists/
    journalism
Merdeka Centre 7
Meyer, E. T. 51
misinformation 3, 39, 48–50
Moore, R. E. 25
music: artists 20, 22, 25; concerts 23–24;
    fans 19, 23–27; performance 23–26;
    popular 24–25; as protest 23–24;
    underground 2, 19–28; in Yogyakarta
    (*see* Yogyakarta)

#NasaanAngPangulo 33, 34

objectification, domestication stage of 49
Ong, J. C. 3
The Onion 8
OnlyFans 41

Pang, N. 3, 48
parody accounts 37–40
participatory culture, concept of 20
Persatuan Sepak bola Indonesia
    Mataram (PSIM) 20, 23–25, 27
Personal Computing/Internet threshold
    (PC/I) 48
Philippines 31–43; *see also* fake news;
    pseudonymous influencers